RIGHT TO CHOOSE?

ACKNOWLEDGEMENTS

My grateful thanks to every woman mentioned in this book, who allowed me to use her story, just as she told it to me, 'if it will help someone else'. My earnest prayer is that it will.

Thank you to the many friends who prayed for and encouraged me, while this was being written. at a particularly difficult time.

To pro-life agencies and friends who supplied or checked statistics and facts.

To Ros, my editor, and the staff of CFP who gave constant encouragement and practical help, I owe a debt of gratitude.

Special thanks to my husband, Eric, who quietly cooked meals and washed dishes in the midst of his equally busy life, and gave me 'space' to write.

Lastly, I thank God for the way in which he has put me in touch with so many women hurting from the trauma of abortion. I only hope and pray that I, through his guidance, may have been of help to them, as they have been to me. It is one thing to read and to know that post abortion syndrome exists. It is another to be there, in the middle of the action, trying to help women come to terms with that trauma. It can only be done with God's help. Writing about it is the easy part.

RIGHT TO CHOOSE?

Maureen Long

Christian Focus Publications

Published by
Christian Focus Publications Ltd
Geanies House, Fearn, Ross-shire,
IV20 1TW, Scotland, Great Britain.

Printed and bound in Great Britain by
Cox & Wyman Ltd, Reading, Berkshire.

Cover design
by
Donna Macleod
Cover image designed by Jim Mortimore
and constructed at Electric Icon
Models: Samantha and Benjamin

Abbreviations

C.P.N.	Community Practice Nurse
S.R.N.	State Registered Nurse, now renamed RGN, Registered General Nurse
M.A.O.Is	Monoamine oxidose inhibitors (anti-depressants)
N.H.S.	National Health Service
G.P.	General Practitioner

Contents

Foreword

As slavery was for the 19th century so Abortion is the great moral issue of our time. Like slavery Abortionism is advanced by those who have a financial interest through the private clinics, where more than half the annual 190,000 abortions in Britain are performed. Like slavery, those who argue for abortionism do so on two grounds, that it is convenient and practical and that it benefits those involved. Like slavery, many of those in the forefront of combating abortion are Christians.

Maureen Long has produced a book that will be of enormous use. For those who are active in counselling the women suffering from post-abortion trauma the book provides guidance and help. For Christians and others interested in the issue in general the book will prove a useful resource. The inclusion of personal stories brings the issue into sharp focus. Abortion is so often swept under the carpet by those who would rather not think about it. These testimonies highlight the legacy of misery and pain for the survivors.

This book is caring, both for the lives that are lost and for the mothers and others who are left behind to pick up the pieces. It is no accident that Maureen Long is linked to LIFE organisation who have, to their great credit, pioneered caring and counselling for those threatened with abortion and those who have been physically or mentally scarred. We must always emphasise that life does not end at birth and that to be truly pro-life we must have a consistent concern for mother and child that goes beyond pregnancy to combat the social conditions and mindsets that allow abortion to flourish.

At the end of the 20th century, Britain is justly proud of its technical and scientific expertise. We have never been so capable of providing for those that are aborted, yet since 1967 we have aborted over 3,000,000 pre-born babies. We are proud of our human rights record, yet with abortion we deny the most basic right of all, the right to life, to the pre-born. We are proud of our democracy, but what kind of democracy removes its pre-born before they are able to ask for a voice? We are proud of our liberties, but what is liberty if we deny millions the liberty to live? We are proud of our tolerance, but cannot find it in our hearts to tolerate the weakest in our society.

The struggle to reinstate a pro-life ethic in society will be long and difficult for it involves nothing less than the accomplishment of a change of heart for us all so that abortionism, like the practice of child execution, withers on the vine in Britain. I fully believe that generations to come will look at the way in which we have squandered the gift of life and regard abortion as an out-moded barbarity. I commend this book as an important step on the road to this outcome.

David Alton

METAMORPHOSIS?

Close my eyes
Disappear
Close my mind
To the fear
Close my heart
To your plea
Close this life
Renew me.
Open my life
To a clean page
Open my mind
To re-engage
Open my heart
But with care
Open my eyes
Future is there.   Or is it?

Meg Matthews

INTRODUCTION.

'I never knew ... why don't they tell you ...' Those two phrases are heard most frequently of all in the pro-life work which seems to occupy more and more of my time..

So, how much do you know about abortion, especially its aftermath? Talking in schools to G.C.S.E. Groups, without exception those opening words are said afterwards. Although told all about the biological aspects of the unborn child, conception and contraception; the true facts of how abortions are performed and their physical and psychological consequences seem to be curiously omitted, unless the pro-life speaker is invited into a school (and that is not always possible because attitudes vary among staff).

Counselling women after abortion, those words are mostly heard through sobs, tears or in agonised voices. Medically, it is possible to go and have an abortion, described, rightly, as a slight operation. What the victims never know, what is rarely told, is the fact that there is a physical and psychological price to pay, with little help available to cope with it.

The national LIFE organisation first realised the need for post-abortion counselling because counsellors found themselves doing it in the course of their 21 years of work. LIFE has a network of offices offering free pregnancy testing and advice. The organisation has also set up residential houses to help pregnant women with accommodation problems. Statistics show that the majority of women find themselves pregnant within a year after an abortion. Counselling those women, especially Life House residents with whom there is a longer contact, it was found that abortion left scars. Some could be healed with another baby to love and care for. Others persisted.

In the United States research was also going on until Post

Abortion Syndrome was officially recognised by the medical profession. There is, at the time of writing, still very little help or counselling offered after the operation by the team of G.P., Consultant, hospital staff, etc., who carry out abortions. LIFE, with the national network already set up, along with other pro-life organisations, are trying to cope with the needs of post-aborted women. With over 190,000 terminations a year, (that is those officially recorded) there are many women silently carrying burdens of grief and guilt which not only blight their own lives, but have a ripple affect on their families and friends. As a LIFE doctor has said, locked away in G.P.s files all over the country, there must be case histories of women who have been treated for depression for years, but have never been offered the therapy they so desperately need because nobody has linked their present problems with a past abortion.

In the following pages, with their full consent, but with names changed, stories of women will be told against the results of the official research published in the last few years. If it helps just one woman to find healing, wholeness and happiness, this book will have been worthwhile.

'My people are destroyed for lack of knowledge' (Hosea 4:6) 'Father forgive them, for they know not what they do' (Luke 23:34).

GROWING

A child
With a child
Within her

Unsure
Immature
And afraid

Alone
And lonely
She's weeping

Abort
Last resort
Cry again

Cherish
Or perish
Decision

Explore
Don't ignore
Find a way

Woman
With a child
Within her.

She knows
Her child grows
To birth day.

Meg Matthews.

PART ONE

CHAPTER 1

'AN INDESCRIBABLE SENSE OF LOSS'

'I feel absolutely abandoned by everyone, even my husband ... That's what they call a woman's right to choose! ... They're all pushing you ... family, doctors, friends, but it has to be your decision ... your responsibility ... then this loneliness ... guilt ... it's never going to end, is it?'

Do you, or anyone you know, feel like that? You may have had an abortion and are unable to understand the feelings which suddenly hit you afterwards. On the other hand, you may have picked up this book because you think that abortion is seen as a quick and simple way out, one in which women get rid of their responsibilities when an unwanted pregnancy occurs. Please read on. Women tell in their own words just what it is like for them.

'I couldn't believe how quickly it all happened. One minute I was having a pregnancy test and then I was just swept along by everyone else. I was worried, well ... terrified ... my father, the doctor, my boyfriend ... they all said it was for the best ... and it was all over ... after a few hours I felt fine ... so they were right ... I could start again. The next day I felt an indescribable sense of loss ... it just got worse from then on ... the depression is always there. It never leaves me.'

Those words, spoken many years afterwards, referred to an abortion on a fifteen-year-old, who did not fully understand what was happening to her, yet they have been echoed over and over. The last thing women expect after an abortion is this 'indescribable sense of loss', yet it invariably hits them like a sledge hammer. If they were prepared for it or even if they could understand the reason why, they would realise that it is not something wrong with them only.

'Until I read your article, I thought I was going mad. Nobody ever says anything, so I didn't think other people felt like me after an abortion,' wrote one lady after the first article on Post Abortion Syndrome which I had written had been published. After it appeared in a national magazine the letters flowed in. Everyone said "Please keep on telling women what it's really like. They don't know!" I did not have to ask if I could use their stories. 'You can quote this if it will help someone else,' appeared on the bottom of most of the letters.

The medical history of abortion over the last quarter of a century has been a curious anomaly. As every doctor knows, when he treats a pregnant woman he is treating two patients, not one, hence the usual scans and concern for the baby as well as the mother. Therefore abortion is the only operation where the object of the procedure is to kill a patient! That is such a revolutionary turn-about by the medical profession that it is even more unbelievable to take in the fact that there is absolutely no follow up, except in rare cases. (At the time of writing, there are only about two counselling schemes set up by the NHS who perform the majority of terminations in the U.K.) In these days when the profession is realising the need for counselling after medical trauma, you can receive counselling after a sterilisation, hysterectomy, mastectomy or any other operation which affects sexuality, but there is a curious omission regarding abortion. Why? Is it because abortion is distasteful even to those medical practitioners who have to carry out the operation now that the law allows it? It seems that everyone, including the patient, wants it to be over as speedily as possible. That would be fine if it were really no more than going to have a tooth out, as has been suggested, but when the feelings described by women surface afterwards, they are totally alone. Is it any wonder that my correspondent felt 'absolutely abandoned'?

Are there sound medical reasons why these psychological disturbances arise?

Firstly, there is naturally a shock to the nervous system. Apart from that when a woman conceives, the new cell, formed from her egg and the father's sperm, contains a fantastic blue-print which determines the baby's physical features and mental attributes, as science has taught us. When a baby girl is born, she also possesses the eggs which will in turn begin the life process for her children. There is therefore a wonderful continuum from a mother to her daughter, who is born with the makings of the grandchildren! Society has always stressed that it is the father who hands down his name, sometimes a business or profession, then his estate after death, thereby continuing the human race, yet he produces sperm as and when needed, from puberty to old age. For the woman, there is a strong, primaeval urge to conceive, give birth and protect her young. For most people, even women who are childless by choice, there are, to a greater or lesser degree, maternal feelings or yearnings from time to time.

Abortion abruptly stops an intricate, natural programme of cell division and multiplication, planned to last throughout the full pregnancy. It also has to be a violent procedure, because the whole pre-birth programme is designed to give the maximum protection to the unborn child. We see this where women sustain falls, serious accidents or illnesses, yet in the majority of cases, still manage to produce a perfect and healthy child. Where abortion occurs, it goes completely against the natural process of growth and protection, as well as disturbing that deep psychological urge to carry on the human race. Is it any wonder that a woman needs to be helped through this trauma as much or if not more than the woman who has a hysterectomy or mastectomy? She is not merely having a clump of her own cells removed. She is losing a child. Until she realises this and is helped to grieve for her baby, there will be psychological disturbance to a greater or lesser degree.

When a baby dies, it is a tragic event in any family. The mother is at her lowest ebb, physically and emotionally. Friends and relatives do their utmost to help and support. Letters and cards as well as visits and flowers are received. There is a funeral, supported by family and friends, a grave to visit on future occasions; a place to take flowers and to shed tears, as we all do after any bereavement in a family. There is a death certificate. Even though it is hard to take in and accept at first, ultimately the mother, the father and the extended family know that a child has been lost. When a mother has an abortion, in the majority of cases there is no support because it is often a closely-guarded secret. Feelings are pushed firmly down, resulting in more psychological problems giving rise to unexplained behaviour.

Margot wrote to tell me: 'We already had a family, growing up, so I had been able to go back to work. I discovered that I was pregnant. My husband threatened to leave us if I had the baby. It was aborted at eight weeks. That was over 20 years ago. It has never been mentioned since ... and I have never been able to forgive my husband or myself. It is like a knife turning inside me every passing year, at totally unexplained moments ... It is such a relief to tell someone ... to write it all down. I thought it was only me who felt this way.'

Once a woman believes she is 'different' because these feelings emerge, she feels even more isolated and unable to share her burden. Suppressed guilt and grief feelings eat away at all that was good and out-going in a person and eventually harden into bitterness. It is not only the woman herself whose life is dramatically altered, but also the lives of other people close to her, including any other children she might have. When you consider that most abortions are done for 'social' reasons, for the financial and otherwise betterment of the woman's life and potential and that of her family, it makes a nonsense of the usual reasons for having an abortion.

Women often decide to abort, like Margot did, to keep a husband or a boyfriend, yet more often than not that relationship breaks up because of the termination. 'I don't know if I still love him ... we just peg along ... for the children ... and grandchildren now ...'

All too often, women find it hard to trust another man or are unable to sustain a physical relationship. Abortion can not only make women sterile, but it can make them frigid for psychological reasons, leading to the inability to have children when they want to.

Margot also wanted to carry on with her career, with her happy family life ... yet she had no interest in her work after the abortion and her resulting depression affected the family happiness. Again we can see that the things she had the abortion to sustain, were still threatened.

'Abortion solves one problem, the unwanted pregnancy, but it throws up many more. Women are never told this. That's totally unfair.'

Dr. Vincent Rue met many post-abortive women in the course of his work at a USA University. He claimed that the after affects of abortion caused severe stress comparable to that suffered by victims of the Vietnam war. His findings are recoerded later in chapter 13.

There is often a delayed reaction, due to the feelings of denial which the woman brings into play, with a typical time lapse of 7 or 8 years after the termination. These women experience growing emotional numbness and disinterest in everyday matters, as in Margot's case. Some, in trying to deny that the abortion happened, use alcohol, drugs or substance abuse to blot out the experience. It does not blot it out. It merely raises other problems, until help is available and a woman is counselled to work through her feelings and deal with them one by one. Sadly, for many women, this never happens and the rosy future she imagined after she had solved her first 'problem', the unwanted pregnancy, never happens either. This is due to two factors. One is the lack of counselling facilities. The other is the fact that women are not told to expect an 'indescribable sense of loss', nor grief, nor guilt, nor any of the other symptoms of Post Abortion Syndrome. Is it any wonder that the depression gets deeper and they are left thinking that the fault lies with them?

Dr. Vincent Rue says: 'Great Britain, with over twenty years of abortion on demand, cannot afford to ignore this looming public health problem. Significant funds for research programmes for national studies are needed together with training programmes for

social workers and the medical profession to begin helping these
women.

In our consumer-orientated society, it is inconceivable that we
have adopted a policy of abortion and never carried out significant
research to study its outcome.'

Most women are left to cope alone, as Tricia in the next chapter.

CHAPTER 2

'I HAD NOTHING TO OFFER A CHILD'

TRICIA'S STORY

'I was over 40 when I discovered that I was pregnant. Throughout my life I had always wanted children of my own, but somehow it was not to be. After I got married I found out that my husband did not like children, did not want children, and could not father them anyway. I felt bitterly disappointed and built up a lot of anger, resentment and bitterness towards my husband, which resulted in my marriage being a disaster from the start. To escape from the loneliness, I began an affair with a man I had known for many years.

'The first time I became pregnant I was still married and my husband knew of the affair and knew of my pregnancy. The desire to have children had turned into an obsession. I was well aware of the risks I was running and did not take the necessary precautions. However, when it actually happened the guilt was terrible - I was pregnant and the father was not my husband. Beneath the guilt, part of me was overjoyed to be pregnant even though I felt that I had no right to be pleased. At that stage, although folk tried to persuade me, I felt that an abortion was out of the question. I was a member of LIFE and I found the whole idea horrific. However, after 10 weeks nature took its course and I miscarried. Despite the seemingly uncontrollable fits of crying that I had, I did feel a certain amount of relief.

'The miscarriage had been physically painful and although I got over that quite quickly, mentally I seemed unable to cope with the wealth of emotions and feelings that welled up. It suddenly seemed as if everyone was pregnant or pushing a pram - why couldn't I? Why had I failed? What was wrong with me? I could

21

not look at babies in prams or watch TV programmes involving anything relating to pregnancy or birth. Soon divorce proceedings were under way and I was consoling myself in an excess of alcohol, tranquillisers and sleeping pills. I never once stopped to ask myself where God was in all this mess. When I began my affair, what faith I once had I threw out of the window. I did not want to feel all the guilt and shame which I was experiencing, so I told myself that if I rejected God then there was nothing to feel guilty about. However, it wasn't until some years later that I realized that God had not let go of me.

'When I became pregnant the second time I was then divorced and living on my own in a small flat. I had given up all hope of ever having a child, because at over 40 I was well aware of the risks involved. Although I denied it at the time, also during the intervening years I was relying more and more on pills and alcohol as a means of escape. Despite that I found myself a job as I wanted to get my life together again after the divorce. The attempt was short-lived because I had to make the agonizing decision about what to do next.

'There was no chance of any support from the father. He in fact subscribed to the 'get rid of it' side. The practical side of me knew that abortion was the only answer, but there was another part of me that said I was about to throw away my last chance of becoming a mother, along with what was left of my feelings for the baby's father. I knew that I could never be with him, but rightly or wrongly, I wanted to have his child.

'Physically, I was feeling better than I had been during my first pregnancy and later on I was to wonder whether, in fact, I would have carried this baby to term. During that time I did confide in a few people, but only on the practical level. They were also people who I knew would opt for abortion. I did not consult anyone from LIFE, as I had the first time. I was determined that I was not going to let any feelings or emotions get the better of me. The desire to keep the child and not to have an abortion was so strong that I did not allow myself to even consider the idea. The facade I presented to the world was one of practicality and "I am doing this for the best".

'I think that the CPN who had been visiting me saw through the chink in my armour, because she asked why I had given up the pills and alcohol when I was going to get rid of the baby anyway. Then I consulted a clergyman. I was hoping underneath that he would tell me that abortion was wrong, but instead he told me that it was 'the lesser of the two evils'. I felt as if I was fighting a battle that was already lost. From then on I seemed to switch to "automatic pilot", sticking rigidly to what had to be done - in case I changed my mind.

'A colleague from work took me up to the clinic in London, where details had to be taken, forms filled in, blood samples given. I was amazed at the number of people there and the way in which the whole thing was being operated like a conveyor belt. It was all in the day's routine! I left at the end of the day having signed the little life away and all that remained was to go through with the actual 'procedure'.

'My ex-husband took me to the clinic where I was to stay overnight. I had refused all help with the payment of the fees because I felt that it was my *punishment* to foot the bill. However, just as I was leaving, my father handed me a cheque for £100 which I was not allowed to refuse. I remained on 'automatic pilot' until we were almost there, when we became caught up in a traffic jam. We were crawling along beside some woods and I had a tremendous desire to get out and run, to be lost in the woods and not have to go through with what I was doing.

'The nursing home was difficult to find and we went round in circles. I prayed (I don't know to whom) that we would not get there. But we did! I was asked if I would like to see the counsellor and although I did not think it would do any good, I said I would like to. I was ushered into a small counselling room, where I had a long wait until she arrived for work. To while away the time I picked up one of those calculators that tell you the expected date of birth. I idly twiddled it round - February 26th - then the dam broke. All the feelings and emotions which I had so carefully kept down, came up. The realisation of what I was doing hit me.

'This was not what I had planned. I wanted to go through the whole thing on 'automatic pilot'. To give in now would be admitting defeat. I was afraid to go home and say that I could not go through with it. When the counsellor actually arrived, I was crying so much that I could not talk to her properly. She asked me if I wanted to go away and think about it, but I knew that if I did I would never manage to go back. She then offered me a single room and said she could arrange for my name to be brought forward on the operating list. That seemed to tip the balance and I agreed.

'I was offered some tranquillisers while I was getting ready, but I refused. I knew that I had taken so many that one more wasn't going to help me. The last thing I remember was lying on a trolley just outside theatre, where I could see the staff all gowned up and wearing Wellington boots. I remember thinking that they would need those boots with all that blood and gore they were dealing with. A nurse asked me if I was sure that this was what I wanted. From somewhere inside me, a voice that felt as if it belonged to someone else, said "Yes".

'When I woke up, I felt quite peaceful and drowsy. I thought perhaps it wasn't so bad after all. Unlike my miscarriage, there was no pain, for which I was thankful. I could hear the girls in the ward next door crying out in pain and I was grateful for my own room so I didn't have to see the agonies they were going through. We had to stay in overnight and were discharged early in the morning before the next batch arrived. It seemed an eternity since the previous morning. I had a beautiful view from my room and I can remember seeing the sun rise big and round over the forest. I thought that all I needed to do now was to get on with my life. It was a lovely morning and I had survived the trauma of the day before. I was quite unprepared for what lay ahead. It was as if part of me had been left behind in that nursing home, part of me had died on that operating table along with my baby.

'When I woke up the next morning the tears started. The peacefulness and optimism that I had felt in the nursing home as I looked out on the sunrise had evaporated and all that was left was a black, gaping hole. I was staying with my parents for a few days and I felt guilty that I was putting them through the agony of seeing me totally unable to stop the tears. It was then that I started on the valium. Every fresh bout of tears and I reached for the bottle until I was in a sufficiently zombie-like state not to care about anything that had happened or anything that was going to happen. About a month later I had severe abdominal pains which I put down to too much alcohol, but when the doctor arrived he abruptly said that it was the evil deed I had done a few weeks before. Those words made me feel as if I had been stabbed with a knife, but I wasn't going to let him see that - instead the angry, aggressive front came up and stayed there.

'During the following months I alternated between doing my job and periods of black depression. Following the abortion I returned to work sooner than the doctor recommended because I could not stand the loneliness of my flat. All the time I kept asking myself where this 'relief' was that they kept talking about. There seemed to be nothing except a total emptiness. Everything I did seemed a tremendous effort. I had no enthusiasm for anything and wallowed in self pity, becoming angry and resentful towards those people who had advised the abortion. During my short pregnancy I had stopped drinking and taking pills, but I was now back on both, together with M.A.O.I.s for the depression. Most of the time I tried to control the drinking so that I could cope with my job, but in the process I became very aggressive and built up barriers around me of being super-confident so that no-one could see the real me which was in bits underneath.

'I hit an all-time low just before the baby's expected birth date. Several things happened about that time. A friend of mine had died in the summer and had left me her collection of soft toys. It was later on that I was to realize the significance of that bit of news! Increasingly I was becoming unable to cope at work and the depression was made worse by the amount of alcohol I was consuming. I was visiting my G.P. on a regular basis and he was keeping me supplied with pills. I was also seeing a psychiatrist and psychotherapist but instead of talking about how I felt, I spent most of my time escaping into oblivion. Several times I had thought about ringing the counsellor at the nursing home. I liked her and she had said that I could ring if I wanted to. However I put it off so long I thought that too much time had gone by and I should be over it long ago. Each time I lifted the phone I lacked the courage to dial her number.

'Christmas was rapidly approaching and I could not work up any enthusiasm for it. I kept thinking that I should have had a little boy or girl to enjoy it with. By Christmas Eve I felt there was nothing to go on for. People did try to help me but I had reached the stage where I refused to listen. I couldn't face another Christmas, so when I went to bed that night I took a large mixture of pills and washed them down with alcohol. I was very angry when I woke up in hospital on Christmas Day and realised that it had not worked. Straight away the aggressive 'I'm all right, Jack' front came up so that no-one would know what I really felt like inside. My overdose brought on a whole new set of problems. I lost my job. I was chucked out of my doctor's practice. I was told they could not help me any more. Three months later I was back in hospital, having overdosed again.

'It was about then that my spending sprees started. I saw a cuddly soft toy in a shop window which reminded me of a cat I once had, so I bought it. After that I went completely over the top, buying soft toys and teddy bears of all shapes and sizes. I told myself that if I had had a child I would be buying it toys, but certainly not as many as I bought. I saw them all as my 'family' and they kept me company in my flat. The toys that had been left to me in my friend's will added to my collection. At the time I think I realised that I was spending far too much, and I knew there was something wrong, but I did not know what it was. It was a tremendous relief to learn later on when I eventually went into treatment for alcoholism and drug addiction, that my compulsive spending was part of the disease of addiction. I also came to realise that in buying teddy bears I was trying to recompense for the loss of my child.

'During the following year I made several attempts to find God amid the mess I was in, but to no avail. I was unwilling to do what was suggested to me and I was not prepared to give up the long-standing relationship with the baby's father. Eventually a member of the clergy who I had been talking to, suggested a Service of Blessing for the two children I had lost. I had to imagine what sex they might have been and think of names. The service took the form of a shortened version of the Communion Service and the two children were placed into the arms of God. At the time I was surprised that I felt absolutely no emotion whatever. Part of me felt that now they were safe in the arms of Jesus, but part of me could still not forgive myself for what I had done. I still wanted children of my own and was full of self-pity that this was not to be. As I look back now I realise that I was totally incapable of feeling anything because I had blotted out any feelings of guilt, sadness or grief with my continuing combination of pills and alcohol. The next few months were a rapid downward slide before I was accepted into a treatment centre for alcoholism and drug addiction over two years after the abortion.

'After the first few weeks of horrific panic and withdrawal symptoms, very slowly I began to change. My attitudes began to change. I started to look at the damage I had caused. I came to accept that I was a sick person trying to get well, not a bad person trying to be good. Now, two years later, my life has totally changed and is still changing day by day. One day at a time I am building my life back together again. I am an active member of my local church and am learning to face life without resorting to the zombie-like existence I was in before. During the early days of my recovery I was still not able to recognise feelings. The combination of pills and alcohol was so effective in blotting them out that even now new feelings are still coming up in connection with the events of the past - my abortion being one of them. Although it was something I talked about during treatment, I did not really feel anything, it was just an event that happened. Now as a committed Christian with a new and wonderful faith, I know that only God can heal that deep inner pain that the trauma of abortion brought me. I feel ready to experience that healing now.'

Today Tricia is still trying to rebuild her life. The bad days are fewer and the good spells longer, as she immerses herself in her Church life, singing in the choir, trying to help other people with problems. She has been through other sadnesses in her family in the past few years, bringing back again the guilt and grief of losing her child, but she has coped without alcohol and pills, although at times it was hard. She has completed a course in counselling and is able to write down her experiences and feelings, praying that God will bring some good out of all her suffering, to help other women to choose life for their babies.

After an article was published in *Christian Woman* magazine in 1989, I heard from women all over the country who had experienced Post Abortion syndrome. They had not been told and were not aware that there would be any adverse psychological effects, therefore thought 'it must be me'. Where healing had taken place, it had always been after a deep spiritual experience, either of conversion or re-dedication to God, feeling forgiven and healed through the cross of Jesus Christ. Even non-Christian counsellors have conceded that 'there seems to be only partial healing without a religious experience'.

Today, many people are crying out for love. The current trend of living together before marriage, changing partners for so-called 'casual sex', and the rising number of marriage breakdowns and divorces, show that many are desperate enough to risk health, emotional upheaval and even life itself, with the risk of AIDS. and other sexually-transmitted diseases, in order to find love. Yet love has been devalued and portrayed as being personal gratification and receiving 'love', rather than as a sacrificial relationship where the well-being of the loved one is of paramount importance.

Is there any wonder that with such thinking, a Man who died on a Roman cross 2,000 years ago does not seem to be the answer to people's needs? Has the church withdrawn into it's own heritage and activities to such a degree that it does not see those who need the gospel so desperately? Where else can the deep, inner needs of a guilty, grieving mother who is not a mother, be met?

Sharon's story in chapter 4, is one that highlights the fact that whilst the medical profession can be found guilty of not 'telling all' as regards the physical and psychological aftermath of abortion, the Church stands guilty of not 'telling all' about the loving and healing work of the Lord Jesus Christ. This can only be a generalisation, and obviously there are churches where the good news of Jesus is taken out and shared in the community, just as there are pro-life doctors, but it is true to say that for the most part the Church expects those who have lost their way in life to come and find it, rather than the other way about.

How different from that early, Spirit-filled church of the New Testament, coping with an equally pagan and violent world, yet boldly proclaiming Christ to those who need to know that someone loves them with a true sacrificial love. How we need to share that in some wonderful way beyond our understanding, the Cross took away all our guilt by putting it on Jesus' shoulders - resulting in healing that gives us the confidence and right to stand before a holy God.

Even today, Suzie, in our next story, cannot confide in members of her church. 'The type of people in my church would just faint to know about me,' she confided. Her story follows ...

CHAPTER 3

'MINE WAS AN ARRANGED MARRIAGE'

SUZIE'S STORY

Suzie was born and brought up in Ghana. At the age of 16 there was an arranged marriage and she was 'sent to England to a man I had never met before.' Her family thought they were giving her a good future by this marriage with a trainee doctor in a Christian country, so they left all the arrangements to the new bridegroom's family and friends. Much later Suzie found out that the person helping with her papers had been asked to add five years to her age, so that when she obtained work in England, she would be paid a higher wage. Her mother had told her that she must obey her husband. Her role was to go to work to help support him through college, then through the first early years of medical practice in a hospital, and with his further studying. The support went on with Suzie working for seventeen and a half years!

Suzie soon realised that living in one room in London, married to and supporting a student husband, was not exactly the Utopia her family had sought for her. She was homesick for them, her home in Ghana and her church there, but knew she must 'obey' her husband, as her mother had requested. Subsequently, when she thought she might be pregnant, just one year later, her husband took control of the situation.

Suzie says: 'I had missed my period for three weeks, but my husband worried that if I was pregnant it would affect his studies. I would have to give up work and we would be in one room with a baby, which would cause a great deal of difficulties.'

Suzie was worried, but even more so when her husband said that although he did not think she was pregnant, she must go to a woman in Holloway who would just 'wash out her womb with

Dettol' - just to be on the safe side. It took a lot of persuasion, but Suzie knew that she had to obey her husband, even though her Christian up-bringing meant that her conscience was deeply disturbed. She knew that it was wrong, but there seemed no way out. At length, she was taken to the woman by her husband and his friend.

'Two days later, I had a period, but the blood was thicker, with clots. I don't think that at the time the full realisation hit me. I just thought of it as my period coming late and brushed it aside. It was only later that the guilt set in. There was never too much time to think about anything, anyway, when she was working full time, looking after their room and cooking.

'I continued working and supporting my husband. Later, we had two daughters, but I still had to work as much as I could.

'When I was 25, once again I missed a period. My husband was still doing further studies.'

By now they had found a flat. Life was still cramped and difficult, but perhaps a little less so because both children were girls and could share. What if she had a boy?

'Again he suggested a termination, but by then it was legal. (The 1967 Abortion Act was in force.) I had days of harassment as he shouted and banged doors, trying to persuade me that it was impossible for us to cope with another child. In desperation, I told a friend who was also a doctor. He said that if I had too many children with a husband like mine, I would live to regret it. I was so angry that I made an appointment there and then with my doctor. The doctor said, "This kind of thing is going to go on every time you become pregnant. I may as well arrange the termination and a sterilisation as well." '

Suzie says, 'My marriage, I think, ended that day. I tried very hard to like my husband, although I had not chosen to marry him, as English women and lots of my friends did with their husbands. Even though it was an arranged marriage, it was our custom and in common with many other Ghanaian women, I did my best to make it work. I had always supported us and had never received a penny of housekeeping money from him. He never ever treated me or the children to anything. I had always tried to accept him as he was, but after that second abortion, I began to find fault with him. I started to hate him, although the children and our friends loved him.

'As the years went on, I screamed inside and did not tell anyone of my constant guilt about these two babies. Later, I began to despise myself for giving all of my youth to a man like him. When my cousin began to seduce me, I gave in and committed adultery with him. I had become hard and bitter and I would not let myself become guilty over my unfaithfulness. It was my way of cheating my husband, getting back at him. I found that I even enjoyed sex outside marriage and tried to tell myself that I had not been married properly in a church. Mine had been a tribal marriage, before elders, yet I knew deep down that it was still a viable one, even though I did not have to go through a divorce in England when we eventually split up. My husband never found out about my unfaithfulness with my cousin, although I think he suspected that something was going on.

'When we finally decided to break up the marriage, I was so eager for him to go that I was the one to find him accommodation.

'As soon as we were divorced, sex did not attract me any more and many times I had to fight off my cousin, even being sexually assaulted by him against my wishes. I had never really cared about men and I have not had any other relationships. I changed my job after going to college after the divorce and have never since invited a man into my home. I have tried hard to live a clean life. I prayed and prayed about all my deep sense of guilt and shame.

'The anger in me against men is great and I feel sometimes that it would make me a bitter woman. I know it is ugly and my daughter said to me, "Stop running men down. You are so bitter. The only man who has ever wronged you is Dad." But even my daughters do not know my full story. I do get lonely and perhaps bitter, but I do not want a man for the sake of it, and yet, who will love me? Even if someone did, my past would rise up like a wave and ruin it. I love my job and many see me as a carefree woman, but little do they know!

'I attend church but the people there would faint to know this. However, God is good and I know that he has the future in hand. My children are growing up and moving away, and I will have plenty of lonely times on my hands. I would like to live them with dignity and be clean. There should be Christian counselling groups. I mean deep counselling as I have carried my guilt by myself for too long.'

Suzie was 39 when she first wrote to me. We corresponded at length. I noted that she continually used the phrase that she wanted to be 'clean'. Most women after abortion feel 'dirty' and used, just as raped or sexually abused women do. Some would argue that arranged marriage could be classed in Western eyes as sexual abuse. Most can sympathise with a young girl, in an alien land, pledged to obey her husband in everything, especially in the marriage bed, yet struggling perpetually against her Christian upbringing and conscience; seeing different Western standards of choice of partner and career etc., all around her, while trapped in her own circumstances, yet not feeling able to seek help at her church.

Suzie worked as hard after her 'divorce' as before, to continue to bring up her girls and make a new life for herself. Her husband lived quite near but never once contacted or wrote to his daughters. A year later he re-married.

I asked Suzie if she had 'given her babies back into God's hands.' She admitted that she found this suggestion helpful, since she had never thought of them 'existing anywhere at all' let alone with God.

I wondered why she had been allowed to have sterilisation at twenty-five, but her papers stated her age as thirty. While she was with her husband she had to keep up that pretence.

When her husband left, he took what furniture and household effects he wanted and broke up the rest. The family were literally on the floor. 'I told the Lord that I was determined to get up off the floor and asked for his help.'

With his help, Suzie once more picked herself up and worked as she attended college. She had done some voluntary work, but needed qualifications to go further. She put her own affairs in order, swearing an oath as to her correct age and reason for the deceit. She passed three 'O' levels and was accepted into college, where she qualified as a rehabilitation officer for the disabled.

'All my bad experiences have contributed to the way I perceive things. They have made me slow to condemn anyone, sympathetic to people's problems and thankful to God. One of my daughters is at University and the other has a good job. One day I would like to live in a house, as I have never had a garden, and of course I would love to afford to go back to Ghana too, and see my mother and the rest of my family, but I am leaving everything to the Lord. I have been far too busy shaping my life, with his help, to feel lonely.

Anyway, I have never known happiness with any man, so do not know what that kind of close relationship would feel like, so I suppose I do not miss it. I just get on with my life with God's help.'

CHAPTER 4

'I'M HAVING MY BABY ADOPTED'

SHARON'S STORY

Sharon was 17, unmarried and pregnant. She contacted the national organisation LIFE, which provides accommodation throughout the British Isles for ladies with unplanned pregnancy problems, and moved into a LIFE House about thirty miles from her home.

There were three other residents, but Sharon succeeded in putting their backs up before very long. As soon as the house-mother arrived for her morning duty, or the evening telephone counsellors came through the door, Sharon would be waiting at the office. I explained to her over and over again that it was necessary to listen to the ansaphone tape first and that meant in private, since LIFE work was confidential, but she could return in ten minutes for a chat. She always did, mostly to complain about the other residents. Someone hogged the bath first, someone else played her cassette player too high, someone else hadn't cleaned the sink properly.

But the main topic of conversation each session was the fact that Sharon's baby was to be adopted. When the counselling team talked to other residents it was the same story. 'She makes me sick. She's always on about how her baby isn't being dragged up in a one-parent family, but by a couple who have worked and saved and tried for years to have a baby. It's going to have everything.'

One evening, when Sharon was being particularly difficult with the other residents and we were trying to bring peace and sense to the situation, she said, 'Why are they so difficult? What are they doing to me? I'm clutching, just hanging on ... to the edge of a cliff and they're pushing me off. It's hard enough to hang on without that.'

Sharon thought she was the one being reasonable and caring,

having her baby adopted, and she was. But it was the gnawing guilt that was making her attitude seem 'holier than thou' to the others who were having an equally difficult time, trying to form 'one-parent families', being abandoned by their boyfriends, coping with budgeting and broken nights.

Obviously Sharon was also punishing herself by giving up her child, feeling she was not fit to be a mother, but trying to make restitution. It was hard for her to cling to that 'cliff edge' and her anger at the other women helped to keep up her aggression towards herself and the whole situation as well.

As we tried to calm frayed tempers and restore personal confidence, we also tried to show the other ladies that choosing adoption as a result of an unplanned pregnancy was a very loving and unselfish thing to do. At least it was giving the child life and a chance, as well as helping a childless couple. Whilst they could understand this, they were fed up with the continual 'bragging' about Sharon's baby's future.

'Methinks the lady doth protest too much,' I quoted one evening to the housemother. 'She'll bring that baby back and keep it.'

However, as the pregnancy progressed, Sharon opened up to me, telling me of her grief when her father died of a brain tumour. She was fourteen at the time and started to smoke, then drift into the pubs and clubs in the nearby city. She also told me every detail of her chats with the adoption officer.

'I can even say whether I want my baby to go to a smoking or non-smoking couple ... and what religion.'

'I think that's lovely,' I answered truthfully. 'I would love to think that while I was in church on Sunday mornings my child was worshipping somewhere else at the same time.'

As my relationship with Sharon deepened, she began to open up about herself. She had told me that the baby was conceived on a holiday abroad. 'I was drunk at the time so I wouldn't know the father if I met him. Anyway, he's foreign.'

Sharon lived in a village and only her mother and grandmother knew that she was pregnant. The rest of her relatives and her

friends had been told that she had come to our seaside town to take
a holiday job for the summer. The baby was due in September,
after which she would return home and resume her former life,
maybe even getting her old job back.

Gradually, the other residents had learned how to deal with
Sharon and even felt sorry for her as she was to give up her baby.
When one girl had a baby only a week or two before her, she had
stayed at the hospital for 8 hours with her, as she went through an
induced labour. The other lady had been brought up in a children's
home and had no relatives to support her. One evening, as Sharon
was telling me of her awe and wonder at being present at the birth,
in spite of her own obvious discomfort, I thought I detected a
glimmer of sadness about the adoption.

'You know, love, you don't have to finally decide about this
adoption until six weeks after your baby is born.'

'I have finally decided. Jason deserves to have the best.'

After a scan had shown that she was expecting a boy, Sharon
had named him. Her Gran had knitted a beautiful shawl for the day
he was to be handed over to his new adoptive parents and Sharon
had bought a little suit for him.

'Every child deserves the best,' I answered gently. 'Different
people look on it differently. Some of our ladies here think that
their own mother love is the best they can give, even if it means
roughing it a bit. Some think that it is a nicer home, upbringing,
education, etc., and that's fair enough, but we want you to be
absolutely sure.'

'Oh, I am. Anyway, I owe it ...' Tears came to Sharon's eyes
and she stopped abruptly.

'Owe it? To whom?'

'To him ... oh you know ...'

I didn't know. 'To Jason?'

'No ... to ... him ...'

'Jason's father?'

'Oh no, he doesn't know ... but I had to ... I had to give him one
back ... to make up ...'

'Who did you have to give Jason back to?'

'To him ...' she whispered.

'Him?'

'Him ... you know ... you call him God.'

'And you feel you have to give Jason back to God because of the other one.'

Sharon was in tears. 'The other ... baby? '

She nodded, then it all spilled out. When she was sixteen, Sharon had had an abortion. She had attended Sunday school as a child, but didn't come from a particularly religious background. She had also seen a pro-life video at school. However, she had been pressurised from all sides to have a secret, quick abortion, although she had already told her friends she was pregnant. She eventually had to give in to that pressure, although she knew she did not agree with abortion.

'The sense of grief and loss afterwards was horrendous,' she confided. 'I wanted the little baby to be a boy and I wanted to call him James, but I knew I couldn't keep him.'

As the tears continued to flow, I knew that the sense of grief and loss, just two years after her father's death, had brought back that earlier bereavement also and compounded it all into a traumatic time.

'After the termination, I stayed in the house for a fortnight, then told everyone that I'd had a miscarriage.'

Statistics tell us that more than half the women in this country who have an abortion go on to have another baby within a year. It is often in the same financial or social circumstances for which they had chosen to abort previously. For some, this second chance of motherhood is enough to heal the hurting. For others it merely accentuates the grief for the lost baby.

In Sharon's case, because she could not deal with her guilt any other way herself, because there was no help at hand, she deliberately had too much to drink on holiday, having planned to get herself pregnant, by somebody who would not know, care, or see her again. In this way she could make restitution by giving a baby to a childless couple. She had heard that one in eight couples are not able to have a baby of their own.

It took me a long time to persuade Sharon that our God is not a God who would ask that of her, but that she could have full and free forgiveness through the cross of Christ.

I went home, sworn to secrecy that I would not tell the other counsellors, praying that the right decision would be made both for Sharon and little Jason.

It is always hardest to confide something the first time. Sharon found that over the next few days she was able to share her abortion experience, first with the housemother, then with her friends at the house, and with other counsellors, but still she remained adamant that the baby would be adopted.

I was amazed when she returned to the LIFE House two days after the birth, having left the baby at the hospital. She cried a lot and told us all how beautiful he was, but she was still firm in her decision.

Ten days later, the housemother was wakened very early in the morning by a telephone call from the house. It was Sharon. 'I want to bring Jason home.'

The housemother, trying to wake up, promised to go and talk it through with her, persuading her not to ring her mother until a more respectable hour! However, once Sharon made up her mind, that was it. A few hours later, after seeing her mother and the adoption officer, she went to the hospital again to see Jason.

Sharon took her baby back to the House and stayed for a week or two, but she was longing to get back to her friends and family. She returned to the tiny village (and the gossip!), but often visits us in the House, and her other friends, now in their own accommodation. She has to travel on public transport, but she loves to come and show us how well Jason is. She asked me to tell her story, if it would help someone else.

Sharon's story shows us the importance of basic Sunday School/Junior Church teaching, even when we fail to keep youngsters in the Church. It also shows us how vital are pro-life talks, videos, slides, etc., in our secondary schools, especially now that the G.C.S.E. Syllabus requires abortion and euthanasia to be covered. It is only fair that the pro-life side is shown as well as the other. However, more can and should be done in our schools and our churches, so that young people like Sharon will be properly informed and better able to make decisions about their own conduct and their future lives.

It would be good to tell you that Sharon now has a new and vital experience of God. That we do not know, but she has accepted the fact that she has been forgiven by 'him' and that she could therefore forgive herself - which maybe is the hardest part for any woman after abortion.

The LIFE Organisation is made up mainly of Christians and within it there are Groups like LIFE Doctors, LIFE Nurses, Evangelicals for LIFE, Anglicans for LIFE, as well as a large Roman Catholic body. But LIFE is not a Christian body in its constitution and ethos and there are pro-life members who would not subscribe to the Christian faith. Therefore Christian counselling takes place only where and when the subject is introduced by the person being counselled, and when guidance is asked for. However, in all the cases LIFE has seen, dealt with, helped over the years, we can testify to the statement made by a non-Christian, that complete healing only takes place when the woman has a true experience that she has been forgiven by her Creator.

Women have a deep inborn urge to give life. Even those women who deliberately choose not to have children go through times when they have thoughts of child-bearing, and to destroy one's own child is a denial of that deep psychological and biological urge to reproduce. Every month, the womb is meticulously and skilfully prepared for motherhood. Every month there is evidence when it has not been needed. Women who abort their babies do feel a sense of guilt and grief that they have committed a crime against the Creator, in whatever form they think of 'him', just as Sharon felt.

CHAPTER 5

'I HATE HIS CHILDREN'

PAULA'S STORY

Paula wrote to me after the Salvation Army publication *The War Cry* kindly published a letter from me appealing for women to come forward with their experiences. She was handed the magazine in a pub. It was because it is distributed in public houses that I asked the Editor to help. After receiving many letters from Christian women who had undergone abortion, I wanted to find those who were not regular Churchgoers. Paula had been through Sunday School. In one letter she quoted John 14:1, giving the reference after 'Let not your heart be troubled.' What faith she possessed, had obviously been a comfort to her, but she still carried a lot of anger and guilt in the two years since her abortion.

'I was over 30, unmarried and living at home with my widowed father. I met a divorced man, who was the father of two children and we started going out together. I deliberately became pregnant four months later, because at my age I felt there was no point in waiting. I have never seen anyone's face drop as much as his when I told him. Then I told my father. Again, the reaction was dismay. "Whatever will the neighbours say with nappies hanging out on the washing line ... and how will you manage financially? It's no good coming to me for assistance."

'There was still my Aunt, my only other close relative since my Mum had died. Her reaction devastated me. She too thought it was best to "get rid of it".

'To this day, no one has ever asked me my true feelings about it. It is a taboo subject.

'Although I knew I was pregnant, it took my G.P. a month to come back with the positive result. (They lost the urine sample!)

43

He had already advised that if I wanted a termination I had better
save up, since I would probably be refused. In the light of all this,
a private abortion was arranged by the time I received an appointment with a consultant at my local hospital.

'I went along to the Pregnancy Advisory Centre for pre-op. and
post-op. counselling, which was excellent, but I felt that I was
paying for sympathy! I was actually booked into the hospital'
(Paula gave the exact time, date, year) 'for part of the morning and
it cost £300, which, to be fair, my boy-friend paid. The post-op.
pain and discomfort was worse than any period pain, but I was told
I was one of the lucky ones; "No cutting, no enforced labour, no
visitors, telephone calls, not too much blood loss. Your periods
should start in a month's time. They might be erratic for a while,
but that's only to be expected. Don't overdo it. Better luck next
time!'

'That last remark made me think of aiming to pass an 'O' level,
rather than avoiding becoming pregnant!

'Two months later my boyfriend had a private vasectomy.
Approaching forty, with two sons, he did not want any more
children. "Save bothering with contraception," he explained.

'We're still together but I don't know for how much longer. I
hate his sons.'

Of course Paula hated his sons! They were alive and her own
baby, equally his child, had been destroyed because she could find
no support from him or her own family. She obviously felt, maybe
at that stage subconsciously, that these living tangible reminders
of his love for his wife were important to him, but not her child,
an expression of their love. This not only made the future of their
relationship erratic, but gave Paula such a sense of non-worth as
a person or a 'partner', not to mention a mother, that she said:

'His ex-wife has remarried and I thought we might stand a
chance. On reflection, I know I made the right decision ... as a
parent I'd be a non-starter. I like my freedom too much ... the

memories may fade as time goes on and the physical and mental pain, but somehow I'll never completely forget. I asked to see what they had aborted. It was brought to me in a jam jar ... I can still smell that smell today ... it was a girl and I was hoping to call her after my Mum who had died four years earlier. Well 'Pauline' the second, I know I failed you, but you'll always be in my memory and you'd have been lumbered with a self-centred mother.'

That was the gist of Paula's first letter, signed, 'An Abortee', but there was an address. She obviously wanted a reply!

After further correspondence and a few telephone calls, with the relationship with her boyfriend 'on and off', we continued to explore Paula's feelings. She had accepted that she would never be a mother and was attempting to rebuild her life, pursuing her artistic interests whenever possible, planning holidays, etc., like any unmarried career person.

Four years later, Paula married her boyfriend. This is a great tribute to her, since statistics show that most relationships, even marriages, break up when the man has persuaded or pressurised his partner into having an abortion. She has now been married over a year and welcomes his sons each Saturday, like many another 'second' wife. She says she has not much in common with them, but knows they have been pushed from pillar to post and unsettled by family break-up and the re-marriage of both parents. As I write, Paula tells me that on reflection she feels that she made the right decision in her circumstances, but with parental or partner support, would have been a mother now. She still gets upset on the anniversary of the abortion, the expected date of the baby's birth, at Christmas and on Mothering Sunday. (This is common with other women who are the victims of abortion.)

In spite of her determination to be happy and make the best of things, it cost Paula a lot to forgive her boyfriend, her father and Aunt, the 'system' which steamrollered her relentlessly on to make an early decision and have the termination, as well as those involved in the actual operation. Her upset shows through the words she used to describe the traumatic day in her life that she will never completely forget.

Society needs to ask just how much legalising abortion has done to women. 'Choice' is offered, yet is it? How much choice is there when everyone seems against you and you are feeling unwell and upset in the early stages of an 'unwanted' pregnancy? Many women have been in Paula's situation, even before the 1967 Abortion Act, and have kept their babies. In spite of all the difficulties, they did not want to do anything illegal.

When abortion was legalized, although it did not become morally right, it gradually became accepted because it was available. It is easy to believe that a thing is right because it is legal, wrong when it is illegal. Did those who introduced and pushed through the legislation for the Abortion Act know that they were letting in abortion on demand? Or did they believe they were stamping out back-street abortion and allowing women the right to choose?

With hindsight, would they have introduced legislation which can cause such unwitting pain, grief and guilt for the women who avail themselves of legal abortion? The whole concept of 'choice' is eroded when women are presented with an option where the only 'choice' seems to be destroying one's own child.

On his third day in office as President of the United States of America, Bill Clinton signed away the pro-life stance adopted by both Presidents Reagan and Bush, with the words: 'We must free science and medicine from the grasp of politics. The American people deserve the best medical treatment in the world. We're committed to providing them with nothing less. Our vision should be of an America where abortion is safe and legal, but rare.'

Fine words, but do they really mean that abortion will be 'rare'? In reality, it means that many more American women will feel that if it is acceptable it is right, and they will be given a 'choice' that is no choice at all.

According to Capitol police, about 75,000 pro-life members turned out to demonstrate their concern. The White House announced that President Clinton had signed memorandums to allow abortion counselling at federally-supported clinics; to permit research using foetal tissue from abortions; to allow abortions at military hospitals and to support funding for overseas population control programmes. He also pledged to review a ban against importation of the French abortion pill, RU486. All of that appears to be helping women to make the wrong choice.

CHAPTER 6

'I FELT LIKE A LEPER'

JANINE'S STORY

For Janine, there was no choice. Under age, the arrangements were made for her, and the abortion was over before she completely understood what had happened. She wrote:

'Let me start at the beginning. I was quite a normal teenager, brought up in a Christian family, who cared for me deeply. When I was thirteen, a close friend of mine had died of cancer and this was my first encounter with trauma. That next summer, my mother began to experience severe pain in the kidney area and doctors were convinced that it was gallstones. Eventually it was discovered that she too had cancer. A few months later she died.

'Understandably, this affected me very deeply. I had become a Christian at quite a young age and my faith was very strong, but these two deaths, especially my mother's, caused doubts to rise up in my mind. About two months before my mother died, I began going out with Kevin, a young man in our church, whose father held quite high office there.

'As my father withdrew more and more into himself with his grief, and because I was a constant reminder to him of my mother, lack of communication made me lean more heavily on Kevin for companionship and love.

'Within a few months we had a physical relationship. I knew that what we were doing was wrong, but as far as I was concerned, Kevin was my whole life and I gave him my undivided attention. At 14, he was my only security. I had lost my mother and my close friend and my father had retreated into his grief. We did not even think of contraception. Almost a year later, I discovered that I was pregnant. That was the worst time I have ever experienced. We had

been to a Christian camp and before we left home I was so worried
that I had a pregnancy test. On my return, I had the result. It was
such a shock, yet a relief to know.

'I told Kevin. He was panic stricken. He told me that if I was
planning to keep the baby he would have nothing to do with me.
You can imagine how my life was again thrown into total
confusion and bewilderment.

'When I arrived home next day, there was a message waiting
for my Dad from the doctor. After my father had spoken to her,
he took me to see her. He showed hardly any reaction. I suppose
I would have understood if he had shouted at me, but this cold
indifference was so hard to take. The doctor arranged for me to go
into hospital two days later. I hardly spoke, I was so scared. I spent
that weekend also in a daze. A nurse asked me all the necessary
questions, but again I was so scared I could hardly answer her.
When she asked me my religion, I felt such a hypocrite.

'She said, "You're very young to be pregnant, aren't you?" and
shook her head. What could I say?

'After the procedure had been explained, I just lay there until
I was taken to the theatre. As soon as I was wide awake again, my
father was there to take me to our lady doctor's house, where I was
supposed to be baby-sitting for her, as she had two young sons. It
had all happened so quickly and I was totally numb.

'On arriving home next day, Kevin's parents came to the house.
His father wanted to remind me how wicked we had been and how
he would have to consider whether to resign his position in our
church.

'Obviously I realised how wrong we had been and was experiencing such deep guilt and shame that the last thing I needed that
day was a lecture. I felt like a leper, knowing that it was too late
for me and my little one. There was just a big ache left. Dad told
me that I must never tell anyone what had happened. I could
understand how he and Kevin's parents felt, although his Dad did
not resign! However, I felt that I desperately wanted to talk to
someone about it.

'Months went by and the subject was never again mentioned. Yet my promise kept me silent. I often thought about what the baby would have been like and envied mothers with their babies, especially those born around the time that mine would have been due. At times I was so frustrated and lonely. I wanted to yell and tell everyone that I had had an abortion, yet the shame and gnawing guilt kept me quiet. When the subject of abortion was raised in discussion, I would shy away, and on occasions when I was asked outright if I would have an abortion, I would feel totally inadequate to answer. How could I give a Christian standpoint and say 'no' when that was exactly the option I had had to take?

'That abortion dominated my mind. I looked for articles in magazines, TV programmes, I searched for counselling groups, etc., so I could share my terrible secret, but there seemed to be no help available anywhere.

'About two to three years later I experienced terrible depression. I could not get the abortion out of my mind day or night. Three girls who had been to our Church became pregnant and kept their babies. Obviously they were supported and admired for not choosing termination, and rightly so, but this made the guilt and grief I felt even harder to bear.

'Also by this time Kevin and I had finished with each other. After the abortion I had been banned from seeing him or phoning him. We met only about every two months, and always under supervision. I longed to talk to him, feeling so alone in my experience.

'To help the depression, I went on a summer camp and there, for the first time, was able to share my secret with a good friend I met. Later, I was to tell only a few more close friends, but it was a very vital part of the healing process and of sorting out my emotions.

'One big struggle which was hard to overcome was that even as a Christian I had murdered an unborn child. Gently, God showed me how much he loved me, yet I could not understand it. Why should he want to use me after I had failed him so badly.

'After four years, I still struggle over the abortion, yet now it is more controlled. My reactions to male company upset me. I hate it if a man seems to look at my body instead of looking at me. Recently I realised how much I need God's guidance because all I have to show for my errors are broken relationships. In meeting men I feel so scared. At the moment I am seeing a lovely gentle Christian man, but I feel like giving up and running away. I feel so dirty. I suppose I dread the day when perhaps I may have the chance to marry but the man would have to know about my past.

'I do so want God to be head of this new relationship, but when my boyfriend visits I am so worried about what I mustn't do that I freeze if he casually touches me or wants to kiss me. I know I should be enjoying his company and not worrying, but it's so hard.

'I know it sounds crazy, but at 14-15 I loved Kevin so much and it broke my heart losing him as well. I suppose no one else will ever be quite so special to me, but I hope that one day I will be able to love and be loved. The physical aspect of a relationship repulses me and I know that would be a big hurdle to overcome if I was to marry.

'Some days are worse than others, but slowly God is helping me and I am thankful for him. He knows all about me and I don't have to explain.'

As we have seen, after abortion women's feelings go through the whole range of emotions. When we lose a loved one, first there is denial. We cannot believe that death has really occurred. As these stories show, sometimes denial can last for several years, then the full impact of emotion hits them. Sometimes it can be overcome.

Once the abortion has been accepted as a 'fait accompli', then anger sets in. Why should it have happened? Why was the pressure there from boyfriend, husband, parents, advisers, etc. That anger has to be worked through, and out, or it turns in, clouding future relationships. Paula was still angry with her relatives, her boy-friend and the abortion clinic staff, then her anger turned on the boyfriend's sons. 'I hate them!' But she was able to forgive her family and accept her position, reach out to the sons and make a new life as a wife, knowing that she would never be a mother.

Anger can only be dispelled with pity or forgiveness, or a mixture of both. Janine could understand her father's grief and distress, therefore she could forgive him his part in it. It was far harder to forgive Kevin's parents because she had taken on herself all the burden of guilt for becoming pregnant, for the abortion, and for jeopardising a church officer's position. Never did she condemn Kevin. She stated matter-of-factly that he said the friendship was off if she kept the baby. The friendship was off anyway and most relationships do break after abortion, where the baby's father has not been supportive. In Janine's case it was parents who parted them, but that did not help Janine to cope. It only helped the parents to keep their 'respectability' in the church, one to hold on to his position and the others to try and put it out of their minds. How can any of them understand how Janine felt or has suffered since?

Hopefully, today we can accept that Christians no longer live in a morally right society; that all of us have contact with the world and worldly values; but that everyone needs love and compassion, especially young people with heightened emotions going through the trauma of bereavement such as Janine experienced with her friend's and her mother's deaths. Hopefully we no longer put 'respectability' before compassion and sweep the dirty washing under the carpet... (to mix a few metaphors.)

Inability to form permanent relationships, frigidity and fear of physical contact is also common after abortion, as it is after rape, along with the feeling of being 'dirty', 'a leper' as Janine described it. How many more like Janine are there in our society, living lonely lives because abortion was freely available?

CHAPTER 7

A CHILD OR A CAREER?

MARION'S STORY: A CAREER

Marion was 34 when she had her abortion in the late 1960s. She told one person only, in strictest confidence, but it was 22 years later when she wrote to me and the pain had not lessened.

'For the first time since it happened, I feel like pouring it all out, with a good excuse to do so. I hope my experience will be of help to someone else. Just to set it down on paper has helped me already. Please accept it in its rough form. I feel I cannot rewrite it. It's done now and that's that.

'When we married, my husband was twice my age. When I became pregnant for the third time, my daughter was 10 and my son 8 years old. I had just completed a 3-year course of teacher training and was about to start my new career. It was a surprise to find myself pregnant again and admittedly I had mixed feelings, for the timing was just not right.

'When I told my husband he would have none of it. Firstly he said he was too old and felt unable to start again with broken nights and all the hassle a new baby brings. Secondly he said that we could not afford another child. We had decided that two children were enough. We had one of each already and he would be retiring age before this third child would be earning. We could not do justice to it properly. Thirdly, I was about to begin a new career for which I had studied hard for three years, while he had supported me financially and emotionally. Legal abortions had just become available on the NHS and I had to make an immediate decision.

'Deep down, I knew that I really wanted to keep this baby, but I also wanted to start my new job, to earn some money and continue our family life as it was developing, with more time for myself,

55

family holidays and all the pursuits of life that a new baby curtails. I know that I wanted to have my cake and eat it too!

'Searching my heart then and now, I know deep down that if my husband had said "Yes, we'll have the baby!", I would have been overjoyed and our lives would have taken a new pathway and we would have coped. But instead he said that unless I had a termination, (we preferred to use that word), then he would leave us, because he could not, would not start all over again with the expense and all that another child would involve. That was his ultimatum. How could I deprive my children of their father?

'Looking back, I know that I should have called his bluff, for I do not believe that he would have left us, although I know that there would have been many difficult times and that the children and myself would have suffered from his ill-humour and verbal abuse.

'Weighing all these things against my own feelings, I allowed myself to go to my doctor and explain the situation. On hearing all my reasons, not my husband's (he did not go with me), he agreed to arrange for an abortion, which was subsequently carried out when I was eight weeks pregnant. The only person I told was my best friend and we have never mentioned it since.

'As the years have passed my decision has lived with me, never really getting out of hand, but yet always there at the back of my mind ready to leap forward at the least hint of a reminder. I have never been able to forgive myself, or to forgive my husband, for forcing that decision on me, although I accept that ultimately it was my decision. My husband is a very forceful person. We have stayed together, although around that time I always thought that I would leave him when the children were grown up and there was nothing for me to stay for, and yet somehow I have never been able to make that break. I cannot honestly say that I love my husband in the way I would like to as a wife, and yet in a way I do love him, I suppose. I can understand that the decisions he has made throughout our lives have been in what he considered to be the best interests of the family as a whole.

'As for my aborted child, he/she would now be 24 years old. It is like a knife turning inside me as with each passing year and at unplanned moments, I imagine what my child would be like, be doing ...and yet life has gone on happily, successfully for me, bringing countless blessings in the form of good health, four beautiful grandchildren and seeing my children in happy marriages.

'My husband and I? Well, sometimes I think we just "peg along", yet at other times we are companionable and reasonably happy, although deep down in my heart I still blame him for what happened.

'Of course, I tell everything to God, without whom my life would have no meaning. However, although I know that he has forgiven me and he understands, I still cannot forgive myself or my husband for what happened all those years ago.'

ANNE'S STORY: A CHILD

Women never forget! At exactly the same time as Marion was pregnant, Anne and her husband decided to have a baby. She, too, had just finished training, in Nursing and Midwifery. She was so thrilled to be pregnant, until, in church one evening after her first missed period, she heard that one of her close friends had German measles.

'A few weeks later, relatives of that friend came to visit. I tried to avoid them. The next day I went to my doctor and asked him to give me gamma globulin, to prevent me getting German measles. He answered lightly that I wasn't even sure that I was pregnant, and dismissed me. I worried for a few weeks until one day I discovered that I did have the disease. My pregnancy was into the tenth week. The dread infection started from my head, sweeping as a rash right down to my feet. I felt so ill and miserable. My husband tried to comfort me, but all I could think of was, "What is it doing to my baby?"

'A young doctor did a house call and was sympathetic: "Why did it have to happen to you?" he asked. A few days later my pastor came and said, "Anne, if the doctors suggest that you have an abortion, go through with it." He himself had been born with an awful deformity. Needless to say, I felt wretched.

'By this time, a consultant obstetrician had taken over my case. He heard my fears and said, "Don't worry! It's already the tenth week. You'll be alright."

'A few days later a midwife friend said, "Oh no! There's danger until the sixteenth week," again plunging me into despair.

'However, no-one advised me to have an abortion and my pregnancy continued. I had all the books to tell me what happened to a baby affected by German measles! By the last month, I felt suicidal! I was thinking, "I cannot bring a deformed baby into the world." No-one knew how I felt though they could sense I was in a crisis.

'One morning I was in church, mulling over the dreadful prospects, when suddenly, a friend gave me a message in tongues and then the interpretation. I knew the message was for me. It was so beautiful! I was not to worry. Everything was going to be alright. My heavenly Father knew of my pain. It was wonderful and I felt free from fear at last.

'A few days later I went into labour and on a Sunday morning, on the last day of the year, I had my baby girl. When she was laid in my arms, she seemed to look me straight in the eye and say, "Well, I'm here and I look alright!"

'I was still worried, but my doctor reassured me she was alright: "Just test her yourself if you don't believe me. She can see and hear." How good God is! Sometimes I ask myself why I had to go through all those months of worry, but I also believe that God protected me from getting the dreaded disease until it was safe.

'Interestingly, my mother also contracted German measles when she was eight weeks pregnant and she also had a normal baby, my brother. She suffered with me, as you can imagine.

'One thing I would advise young women: Make sure that you are vaccinated against German measles before you decide to start a family.'

Anne wrote from Addis Ababa and concluded, 'A few days ago we received a beautiful photograph of our daughter as a bridesmaid at a friend's wedding. She has been our pride and joy all these years and we praise God for her. We didn't have any more children, although we both longed for them.'

Marion has mourned a 'lost' child for all of the years that Anne has been thankful that she went ahead with her only chance to have one. The availability of abortion causes pregnant women heartache which was unknown before.

CHAPTER 8

IT'S A NIGHTMARE!

Is abortion ever justified? For rape? For handicap?
Many people, including some Christians, would say that abortion is ethically wrong except for some 'hard' cases. It is this body of opinion which 'sits on the fence' and slows the pro-life movement. Ironically, they believe that they are showing a caring, Christian attitude towards the woman who may, like Anne, face bringing a handicapped child into the world, or, if a rape victim, will bear the child of the 'monster' who raped her and haunts her dreams.

For the woman concerned, whatever the cause for the abortion, the aftermath still takes its toll. Even the rape victim is bearing a child who is genetically half her own, who, if he or she is destroyed, will be a classic case of retribution for 'the sins of the fathers', by his or her own life being denied. That is hardly Christian justice and love! Apart from that, the trauma of an abortion after the trauma of rape imposes a double vicious toll on the rape victim. A birth, even if adoption follows, is the more therapeutic for the woman's eventual psychological healing.

For Marion, who just 'pegs along' with her husband, life is 'second best'. Only by her own forgiveness, tolerance and loyalty is her marriage still functioning, albeit not in a perfect way.

Liz, too, had a forceful husband who said abortion was the only solution, but she did summon up the courage to oppose him. 'Does that make me a bad wife or a sane and sensible woman?' she asked. After standing up to her husband, she went through a pregnancy and birth with verbal abuse from him.

'His sadistic language towards me was recognised even by the maternity hospital staff, who would draw the screens around me at visiting times when the other women had loving and attentive

61

husbands with them. I was allowed to have my baby to feed or cuddle, to comfort me. Her birth had been traumatic. An hour before, everything seemed to seize up. My first child was only 11 months old when she was conceived and I suppose I suddenly realised that everything was so wrong: my husband's attitude, two babies dependent on me, the nightmarish verbal abuse. My muscles tensed as I told myself I could not possibly have this baby.

'It must have been a dreadful struggle for her to be born, but there was a super midwife who helped me through a terrible confinement. It was all worth while a year or two back, when my daughter's fiance, now her husband, on their Engagement day, put his arms around me and thanked me for her. I would not have missed that for anything! I know that all the time God has been there to help me through. Underneath are his everlasting arms.'

In spite of the evidence of the trauma of abortion, still many support it for these 'hard cases'. The Church of England Synod this year (1993) failed to produce an outright pro-life stance. Its Board of Social Responsibility amendment, while agreeing that there were too many abortions, still stated that, where necessary, they should be carried out as early as possible and when, in rare cases, after 24 weeks, it should only be on a handicapped baby whose survival is 'only possible for a very short period'.

If a baby is only expected to survive for a very short period after birth, why play God and hasten the process? Doctors have been known to be wrong before. Won't women always have niggling doubts? What if ...

One Christian lady wrote: 'Nearly three years ago I had an abortion because the baby I was carrying was a Down's Syndrome. We already had two lovely daughters aged six and four. Although I was a Christian, I was unable to face the prospect of a handicapped child.

'The doctors at our local hospital said they had never seen a baby which looked as this one did on the ultrasound screen. They were interested enough to send the baby for a post mortem after the abortion. I was told that as well as the chromosome abnormality, the baby was not properly formed inside and would not have lived anyway. This was supposed to make me feel that my decision not to have the baby was justified.

'What I actually felt was very different. There was no pressure put on me by anyone to have the abortion. Rather, I felt totally abandoned, even by my husband. Everyone said that this must be my decision (implying that then they could not be blamed afterwards).

'As the pregnancy had gone on for nearly five months, the baby had to be 'born'. The nurses and doctors did what they could to be kind. I was allowed to hold the baby, but all I wanted by then was to blot the whole thing out of my life. I could not bear it. The grief and loss were real, but I felt too ashamed to talk about it to most of my Christian friends. I had very few people to help me. The fact that the baby would have died anyway accentuated my guilt, as I felt that I could have left everything in God's hands and he would have dealt with the situation.

'For some months I lived with the guilt and grief and loss, then the Lord intervened. I was baptised in the Spirit and I knew that I was forgiven. I do not believe that there was any other way I could have been healed. Of course I have not forgotten what happened, but the awful sense of guilt has gone. I promised the Lord that I would never have another abortion and I pray that he will not allow me to become pregnant again.

'I would have been so glad to have someone to talk to when I felt so awful. Recently I went to my G.P. to offer myself if any other women wanted help. He was very discouraging. I feel that there is a need for counsellors in this field, but surely they need to work with the medical profession, like the Society for Stillbirth and Neo-Natal Death (SANDS) does. Locally, we have a Pregnancy Crisis Centre, but few doctors give approval or practical support.'

Sadly, with a few exceptions, that is usually the case.

Liz, who resisted pressure to abort, is herself a SRN, or RGN as they are now called. She had an experience which brought her own feelings back to her, when she was working on night duty in a residential home for the elderly. There was a resident catering assistant, who would often walk the grounds during the night, or talk to the nurses in the staff room for hours, because she could not sleep. Later, it transpired that she had had an abortion six months before and was having recurring nightmares. Since she slept across the corridor from her boss, she could not risk her screams being heard. Brought up as a Roman Catholic, she had lived with a man for several months. After the abortion the relationship had broken up.

Nightmares and screaming are not uncommon for woman who cannot come to terms with their abortion. Margo wrote:

'When I was three years old, my father left my mother with me and four older children. He was, and I believe still is, a Satanist, worshipping the devil as the prince of darkness and denying the very existence of heaven. I was not old enough to understand this and the loss I felt by his leaving was an ongoing pain for years and years. It was a heavy weight inside me, and as I lay in bed each night, I would long for his return. Even though he had never shown me any affection, in my vague, snapshot memories of him, I still longed for him. He was my father.

'I grew up afraid of men and would clam up in their presence. As a teenager, I found relationships with boys difficult, and could not keep a boyfriend. Then I met Rob, twenty years older than I and married with children. His wife had left him. I fell in love with him, the father-figure for whom I had longed for years. When I became pregnant by him, I was only eighteen years old. I was shocked to hear that he did not wish to start a new life with me. I had only been someone for him to console himself with, because of his broken marriage. He decided that I must have an abortion. He said he would find the money for it somehow.

'I told my mother I was pregnant, hoping that she would help. All she seemed afraid of was what the neighbours would think! She also said that an abortion was the best thing for my "problem".

'I felt completely alone. Everything seemed unreal. It surely couldn't be happening to me? Because I had always had irregular periods, I was found by a G.P. to be five months pregnant, too late for a "simple" abortion. The doctor, too, recommended an abortion, since the baby's father was a married man. I was in a daze. Surely these people all knew best. I told myself that I must listen to their advice.

'The doctor said that he would arrange for me to have the "termination" on the NHS. He said I was very fortunate that he was able to help me in this way. I was sent to the consultant who examined me and while I sat there in a daze, told me I would need a hysterotomy. He barely glanced at me as he gave the second signature, required by law, to the green form my doctor had already signed.' (A hysterotomy has to be performed when the baby is too advanced for the more usual suction method used in abortions of babies up to twelve weeks gestation. It is like a Caesarean birth, but the baby is mostly too tiny to survive. Anyway, should it survive the operation, it is left to die because that was the purpose of the procedure.)

'Soon after this I was admitted to hospital and the termination took place. Afterwards I remember feeling a slight relief that it was all over. Now I could go back to my life. I was sure that Rob would get a divorce, since his wife had left him, then we could get married.

'In reality, Rob's wife went back to him and I had to try and get on with my life alone again. That was when the nightmares began. Night after night I would scream and scream. My mother would tell me about it. At first, I was unaware of it. I would wake up every morning with a painful throat, but the screams were so loud that they woke up the neighbours and they began to complain. Sometimes I woke up or my mother woke me up and I found I was out of bed and banging on the bedroom window. I'd be confused and go back to bed panic-stricken. I did not know what was happening to me.

'Then I met Rob again. His wife had left him once more, for good this time. He said that he loved me and wanted to marry me.

He too had regrets about the abortion.

'For the next three years we lived happily together, although the nightmares continued. Now it was a way of life and we both accepted it. It was difficult to go on holiday or sleep away from home as we needed detached accommodation. Deep inside me there was still a heavy weight and it was growing worse. I'd wake up in the night and wonder if there was a God. If so, how could I explain to him if I had to meet him at a Judgement day, if there was such a day, about my abortion. That weight just grew heavier.

'Rob and I were married and I gave birth to a lovely baby girl. This made the nightmares worse for a time. I saw and held in my arms "what might have been". Rob and I did not discuss the abortion, but we knew that I had very deep regrets. Again, the nightmares were a way of life.

'When my little girl was eighteen months old, I gave birth to our son. For a while I seemed better. I felt fulfilled by my babies. It was as if the second baby replaced the aborted child. The nightmares were less frequent, yet that weight was always there, a reminder of my dark past.

'Then, about seven years ago, I saw an advert in a magazine. It showed Cliff Richard holding a booklet called *Power for Living*. He explained in the advert about his relationship with God through Jesus. The booklet was free and no money was to be donated. This attracted me, because I was convinced that churches were only after your money. I sent for the booklet.

'When it arrived, I read about how Jesus had died on the cross. It gave a simple prayer at the end, to invite Jesus into your life. It suggested asking Jesus to forgive specific sins. I knelt down on my bedroom floor that afternoon and asked him to forgive me for having an abortion. I thanked him for dying for me and asked him into my life. I didn't feel any different. I just got up, feeling glad that I'd done it. Then I more or less forgot about it and carried on as before.

'A few weeks later I suddenly noticed how beautiful the fields and hedges looked. I heard the birds singing. It was lovely. I noticed the sky, too, and how bright it was.

'In the booklet I had received, there was a tear-off postcard, to send off if I decided to accept Jesus as my Saviour. I had done this and months later a new booklet arrived, called *Steps to Christian Maturity*. It mentioned the importance of reading the Bible regularly, so I decided to do that. I had read John's Gospel when the first booklet came. Now I began Luke's. When I came to chapter 7, with Jesus dining at the house of Simon the Pharisee, I identified with the woman who came in off the streets and wept at Jesus' feet. The abortion weight was so heavy and I became that woman. I wept and wept as I read of how Jesus had said, "Go in peace. Your faith has saved you. Your sins are forgiven." I knew that he was speaking to me.

'When I woke up next morning, I was amazed to find that heavy weight had left me. I no longer felt guilty. I joined the local church and was baptized. Through my experience and the difference in my life, Rob has also become a Christian. Now I live each day for the Lord. Nothing that I can ever do can repay him for all his love has done for me. Like the woman in the story, I love him a lot because I have been forgiven a lot.

'Today, I feel angry that the Church does not speak out at the shedding of the blood of the innocents. But more than that, my heart grieves for the women who are being deceived by society, being told that it is alright to have an abortion. Like I was, they are led to believe that society is right, that people who make such decisions are intelligent, well-informed leaders.'

Margo, who had no Christian upbringing, had to find out the hard way, but an advertisement in a popular magazine attracted her, because Cliff, a well-known person, guaranteed that Jesus could solve life's problems. Margo was ready to try anything. She discovered that only God can bring about complete healing for the deep wounds of abortion. Finding freedom from years of nightmares certainly gave her a new life. Finding freedom from the weight of guilt and grief was an unbelievable bonus.

There are those who say that Post Abortion trauma (or syn-

drome) is a condition imposed on women by Christian indoctrination or pro-life propaganda. Margo's story gives the lie to this.

After an abortion, almost every woman finds a temporary
relief. It is the 'indescribable sense of loss', the overwhelming
guilt that suddenly surfaces afterwards that none of them are
prepared for, whether or not they were one of the 'hard cases'.

One of the hardest of the 'hard cases' must surely be incest. Is
abortion justified for this? Celia wrote:

'I was very young when I was assaulted by a member of my own
family. No-one thought I could be pregnant, but I was. The adult
members of the family swiftly arranged an abortion, and assumed
I was too innocent to know what was going on. The trauma of the
act of abuse plus the trauma of the abortion had a dreadful effect
on me. I was a bright child but my schoolwork suffered. "Celia
should concentrate more." "She can do better!" Afterwards, such
comments appeared on my reports. Later my parents separated,
then my mother died of cancer. All this compounded until I was
having to see psychiatrists and was eventually diagnosed as having
multiple personality. Wrong handling of my feelings when I was
young and abused and confused helped to bring on the bouts of
mental instability.

'Later I married and our first child was born. I became ill again,
having to spend time in the local mental hospital and for the
following thirty years I struggled with poor mental health.

'I was in my fifties when I again became very ill and was
admitted to a psychiatric hospital. Here I had skilled counselling
and for the first time since the abortion and the assault I was able
to face those repressed memories.

'Members of the Church family and my Vicar supported me
greatly and I began to accept that what had happened was a part of
my life I had to face. Some time later the memory of the aborted
baby rose in my mind and I was able to begin the grieving process

for him. I wept for him that day as if it was the day I had lost him. Although so young, the memories had stayed in my subconscious mind. My baby had lived for a few moments and I had heard vaguely what was said, through the clouds of anaesthetic. I knew it was a boy and I named him in my mind. It was many years later that I was able to have his name written on a piece of paper and placed on the altar for a communion service. Without him being named publicly, he was prayed for and 'given back' to God. I felt that for the very first time in all those years he was acknowledged as a real person, my lost son, whom I would meet one day in Heaven.

'When I was beginning my nursing training before marriage, I was present at the death of a 7-year old boy. I never got over that death till twenty years later, when I was able to weep for him. It had affected me so deeply, firstly because it was the first death I had witnessed, but mostly because I knew he was the same age as my son would have been. Every woman I have talked to who has had an abortion has said, "He/she would be such and such an age now." Every abortion leaves a potential mother.'

It has taken many years of patient counselling and heart-searching for Celia to come to terms with her past and forgive the close member of her family who abused her. She lost the first 30 years of her marriage and motherhood, with constant mental health problems. She was never able to have more than her one child, yet she knows she is the mother of two. She said, 'I believe that not just from the moment my son died by abortion, but from the very moment of his conception, he was firmly in God's loving care.'

For Celia, abortion was not the answer to her 'hard case'. Instead it cost her years of her life. She confided, 'I have read many arguments against abortion, but few seem to consider the feelings of the mother after the child has been aborted.'

Like us all, she has also read many arguments for it, especially after incest. But like other types of rape, one trauma just compounds another. Forty years of your life is a long time to pay for the 'solution' to a problem, that was arranged for you by other people. Sadly, in spite of stories like Celia's, many people still think that it is the only answer.

Rape is the most common 'hard case', quoted in arguments for abortion, but a very sad letter to a magazine read as follows: 'Ever since I was raped three years ago and had an abortion, I've felt as if I have been going mad. I never saw the baby but I dreamed about him for months afterwards and now I cry because I didn't allow him to live. It wasn't his fault that I was raped - he was an innocent little baby. Now my obsession with babies is getting out of hand. I have started thinking about snatching someone else's. The other day I saw a mum with several scruffy children and a baby in a dirty old pram. It was as much as I could do to run home and get away from the temptation to grab the child. I know I could look after that baby much better than the mother can. Now I'm frightened to go out because all I do is look at babies and wish they were mine. I am scared to admit my feelings to anyone in case they report me to the police and I get arrested' (*Take a Break* magazine) .

How sad that this lady wasn't given enough of the right counselling. She realised too late that her little one was not responsible for his father's actions and should never have had to pay with his life.

Once denial and anger have been worked through, forgiveness is the next great hurdle for the woman who has had an abortion. It is the most difficult thing in the world to forgive.

First husbands, boyfriends, parents, doctors, nurses, consultants, friends, relatives, in fact anyone who pressurised or helped facilitate or perform the abortion. Women are encouraged to use many ways to help them forgive. Letters can be written and torn up. People can be approached face to face or written to. It is always painful to admit that you forgive someone. It can upset them more than the person doing the forgiving. One young lady wrote to the surgeon concerned and asked him not to do any more abortions. She never received the courtesy of an answer. The next step is often to ask the baby's forgiveness, in an attempt to help a woman to forgive herself. Some women have written a letter to the baby. For some it is enough to name him/her and 'give them back to God' either in prayer or in a service such as Celia experienced. Some pastors, ministers, clergymen will arrange this after an abortion has been disclosed in counselling. The service does not have to be public, but the mother is comforted that her baby has been acknowledged. An aborted baby does not have a funeral or a death certificate. The mother does not receive sympathy cards, flowers or comfort. It is as if her child has never existed. It is only by acknowledging that existence and accepting the child as a real person, that the healing, grieving process can begin.

Many women need to know that God has forgiven them, as we have seen. For many more, the greatest stumbling block is the inability to forgive themselves. Jackie said: 'I had an abortion eleven years ago. I wasn't a Christian at the time, but I will never forget the heartache I went through. I felt that I had committed murder. I cried and cried ...

'My husband and I had been separated for a few months and having the termination was his condition for having me back. I went through life like a zombie until I had another baby.

'I loved that baby so much because I felt that she had taken the place of the first one and I tried to forget what I had done. The pressure he put on me to have the abortion made me hate my husband and we finally divorced four years ago. After that I became a Christian and God has his ways of healing our lives. Eventually the abortion came up and after having confession and absolution, I felt that I had finally come to terms with the guilt and could be free of it.

'However, a few weeks ago, during an argument, my mother threw the whole thing back at me. I felt the hate rise again for my sister, who had pressurised me into it as well. My new-found peace was shattered. Then two good Christian friends passed on to me the copy of *Christian Woman* magazine with your article about abortion. My new husband, who is also my best friend, talked it all through with me and we prayed about it. We prayed about my feelings for everyone involved, and that helped.

'But the thing I really felt I should pray for, which I had shut out all through the years, was the foetus. I had always thought of it as a lost soul, wandering around on its own. But it was with God who would love and care for it.

'It had bothered me for some time that there seemed nowhere for women to go and talk over their problems after an abortion. People think it is the solution to a problem, but fail to realise the number of other problems that it throws up. It is marvellous that the LIFE organisation can provide that service and that women can turn there for ongoing counselling.'

'Mourning is too petty a word for what people go through!', says Frances, who was expecting a child of a man whom she cared for but did not love and who wasn't free to marry her anyway.

'When I discovered that I was pregnant, I was in hospital, in the Isolation Ward, with gastroenteritis, pancreatitis and salmonella. Although the nursing staff were wonderful, I was very much on my own, with no counselling or understanding to help me make up my mind about the termination. I was definitely not warned of the trauma suffered afterwards.

'I went ahead with the abortion in early Autumn. The date is still very vivid. I can remember coming round from the anaesthetic feeling very bruised and confused. The next morning I was discharged to go back to work.

'The months following were more painful than anything else I have ever experienced, even in bereavement. Guilt and shame are probably the most overwhelming of the feelings which took over me. I felt that I was a murderer, cruel, callous and uncaring.

'Everywhere I looked I saw pregnant women, young babies and children. The sight of any of these were enough to send me bolting for a hiding place, where I would sit until I had rationalised my feelings. It was impossible to live a normal life. I told myself that I had done the right thing, that I could not have brought up a child unmarried and alone. It seemed never-ending.

'Yet time does heal and now the only time it affects me is the date of the termination, the expected date of birth, Christmas and Mother's Days. It is not a thing I am proud of, but it is not a daily horror now.

'Until I read your article I thought that an experience I had was just crazy. Possibly a year after the termination, I had a very vivid dream, in which I saw my Grandmother and my child, holding hands. She said, "I've got him. He's safe." Now whether this was just a fanciful dream my sub-conscious was using to make me feel better, I don't know. I'd like to think not.'

In the article, findings from Dr. Anne Speckhard's research were listed. She made a study on the long-term results of post-abortion stress, taking women who had aborted approximately five to ten years before. She found that:

81% were continually preoccupied with the aborted child.

73% were haunted by flashbacks of the actual abortion experience.

69% had feelings of going crazy.

54% had nightmares relating to the abortion.

35% had experienced 'visitations', from the aborted child.

In her book, *Abortion, A Woman's Birthright?*, Christian writer Noreen Riols describes her own dream of her aborted child, safe with Jesus. Many other women have told me that they have dreamed of a parent or a grandparent, no longer living, who have appeared with a child, which bore the family likeness, in a dream. Is this, as Frances wonders, just the sub-conscious playing tricks because women want to believe that their aborted babies are safe in God's hands, with other loved ones who have passed on, or is it God's special seal of healing for aborted women? We only know that the Bible tells us that God knows us intimately from the moment of our conception (more of that in the section on the Biblical stance on abortion). The fact that over a third of long-term stressed women 'see' their child in a dream afterwards, could lead to the conclusion that in some cases this is part of divine healing. After all, what is the 'sub-conscious'? Who governs it? [1]

'Frances had become a Christian at a very young age, and was an active member of her church until she joined the Army.

'With life so very different there, I became a backslider. For three or four years I virtually never went to church or had anything to do with Christians. Mainly because of the termination, I felt too unclean to go into a church, too much of a sinner ever to be forgiven.

'Thankfully, over the last two years, through going back to church and through starting again to read the Bible, I know that God has forgiven me and that through my experience I am a far stronger Christian, working daily for the Lord.

'Mourning is too petty a word for what people go through after abortion. I read your article with tears streaming down my face. Putting pen to paper about it is not easy. I don't know what the answers are.

'In my job I see many young women pregnant and scared. Their decision cannot be made for them, but at least I hope that by sharing my experiences and guiding them to professional counsellors, their choice is helped and they won't go through the pain that I experienced.

'I'm still unable to refer to the termination as an abortion. The pain will always be there with me, although eased over the years.

'The time has come for the community at large to know that it is never an easy way out and that women need trained counsellors to help.'

---

1. More recently, doing a pro-life training session for a new Church Counselling Group, where this was mentioned, a lady came up to us afterwards and told of a similar experience after a miscarriage. She had seen her Gran in a dream holding her baby and said it was the comfort and healing that she so badly needed and she was grateful to God for it. (I would be interested to hear of any other instances of 'dreams' like this.)

SUGGESTED WORKSHOP /
DISCUSSION GROUP / PRO-LIFE SEMINAR

1. Leader reads Frances' story, either live or puts it on tape.

2. Each member of the Group to think themselves into a character involved or who could be involved, i.e. Frances, one of the Isolation ward nurses, the doctor who confirms/discovers her pregnancy, her boyfriend, mother, father, best friend, senior officer in the Army, etc. Choose your character as to what fits your age, sex, experience. Obviously if this is a large group, smaller groups would need to be formed. Take ten minutes to do this, prayerfully, and write your notes.

3. Discuss your findings. Explore your own feelings, whether it changed your preconceived ideas, expanded your knowledge, gave you a greater understanding, etc.

4. Bible work.
Read Psalm 139; Jeremiah 1: 4-5; Isaiah 49: 1, 5, 6.

5. Prayer
Thank God for what has been learned in the session.
Thank God for the healing which Frances has found.
Pray for anyone contemplating abortion.
Pray for anyone who has had an abortion today at your local hospital.
Pray for the work of the local pro-life organisation that those victims will be led to them.
Pray for anyone you know who has had an abortion and needs healing, in silence if necessary.
Ask God to show you areas of healing and opportunity, witness and influence in the areas in which you move.

6. Discussion: Ask yourselves what you can do:
a) As individuals.
b) As a group.
c) As a church
d) As a Society?

Conclude with the Blessing.

CHAPTER 9

'THEY ONLY WANT YOU FOR SEX!'

KAY'S STORY

In a society where sexual achievement is held as the ultimate, where love is devalued and physical gratification has superseded the need for emotional and spiritual fulfilment, it is perhaps not surprising that a child, the result of conception, is deemed expendable and of little worth. Women who have had abortions because their partners have abandoned them when they became pregnant, can be forgiven for thinking that all that men want from them is sex. It appears that most post-abortive women either experience frigidity, a fear of being touched in any way, problems with their future sexual activities, or else they feel of so little importance and crave so much for 'love', that they decide to 'have a good time' and proceed to go through a string of sexual partners. Kay chose the latter course.

'I became pregnant when I was just 17, after my first sexual relationship with a young man.

'I was living at home with my mother and step-father. All my family, except for my father, turned against me, when they knew that I was pregnant. They really put pressure on me to have an abortion. I wanted to keep the baby, but I was extremely confused and frightened, with no one to turn to for help.

'The baby's father had left and I did not know where I could contact him. It was more or less decided for me that I was to have an abortion. I was admitted into an NHS hospital.

'I had an extremely nasty experience at the ante-natal clinic, where the doctor who was to do the termination treated me roughly, especially during an internal examination, when he hurt me a lot.' (This could quite easily happen where a woman, having

77

her first 'internal' is terrified and tensed up anyway. Doctors and nurses need extreme sensitivity and care, but they see so many ... and do not always deal with their patients' feelings as well as their bodies).

'The Ward sister at the hospital advised me not to tell any of the other patients the reason why I was there. She need not have worried! I hardly spoke to anyone whilst in hospital. I was too shocked and scared. Those next few days were like a nightmare. I can remember every detail of the preparation, then being wheeled to the theatre.

'I felt that I wanted to die with the baby, because I did not know how I would ever cope with the pain of it all.

'After the operation, my family came to visit me. Their attitude towards me was completely changed when they knew that I had 'got rid' of the baby, as they put it. As far as they were concerned it was all over and they had come to "cheer me up", as though I had just had my tonsils out or something! It still hurts me to think of their lack of respect towards my feelings and their lack of understanding about what I had done and how bad it had made me feel, not to mention their lack of respect for the life of my child.

'When I was discharged I was not told of any counselling there might have been. I was just given an appointment for the six-weeks-after check and that was that.

'I think the first feelings I had in the next few months were ones of guilt. I was continually crying or on the verge of tears, for the slightest reason. I couldn't bear to look at babies and wouldn't get involved with them at all.

'I became very depressed in the Spring of the following year, around the time that my baby would have been born. After that I tried to stop thinking of it as being a baby and tried to think "foetus" as it seemed less real.

'Even though I started working full-time, I didn't really have any friends and I remember I desperately wanted to tell someone. Eventually I told the first man I went out with after the abortion, but it didn't help.

'I found relationships with men very difficult. I was feeling extremely insecure, yet wanted desperately to be loved. It seemed to me that all men wanted was sex, so that was what I gave them, although I never enjoyed it. I thought it would make them love me, but I always ended up hurt. I drifted in and out of relationships, trying to kid myself that I was having "a good time".

'I had many bouts of deep depression and I also started to drink quite heavily, after I left home, when I was twenty.

'I met my husband, Dan, five and a half years after the abortion. I felt secure with him. We fell in love and started living together.

'Still, it wasn't easy. I continued to have bouts of deep depression. He had problems of his own and it proved quite a stormy relationship. Two years later, I began to feel a strong urge to have a baby. It became almost an obsession. I felt that it would be the only thing to make my life mean something.

'I became pregnant and as the pregnancy went on, I also had a strong urge to go to church. I had been baptised into the Catholic faith, but my Catholic up-bringing stopped when my parents divorced when I was 10 years old. Because I was pregnant, we managed to get a Housing Association flat. I plucked up courage and went a few times to a nearby church, which I really liked.

'Our daughter was born in the July. A few weeks later my husband, after being involved in a road accident due to his drinking and driving, ended up in hospital. I think it was then that he decided to give his life to Christ. We both started going to church and a few months later, after we chatted to the Rector about our baby's baptism, we became Christians. As soon as possible after that, we were married.

'Because of my past, I found the Christian life a real struggle. I felt even more guilty about my abortion, knowing how a Christian should feel about it and whenever the subject came up I became confused and upset. I was still suffering from fits of depression and was having Christian counselling for that. We prayed about the abortion and although I felt forgiven by God, I still hated myself and my family for doing it.

'The turning point came for me in the New Year, when the David Alton pro-life Bill came to everyone's attention. I became very defensive and felt it would be hypocritical for me to take a stand against abortion.

'Our Rector preached a sermon on it. I made myself go to church that day, but it was very hard to sit and face up to facts which I'd always pushed out of my head. After the service, the Rector talked to me and asked if I would attend a *Care for Life* meeting the next evening. I said I would, but all next day I kept hoping that something would happen to prevent me going. But God obviously wanted me there! I went with the Rector and two close friends.

'That was one of the hardest things I have ever done, but that night I received Christ's healing.

'I thought women like me would be condemned by all the pro-life Christians, but instead they were full of compassion. It was terrible to hear in graphic details the horror of abortion, but it was the first time for years that I had thought of my baby as a baby and could grieve for her. At the end, they dropped two million white petals to represent each of the lives lost by abortion. I realised that one of them was for my child!

'The next few weeks were hard, as I mourned for that lost baby, but I was comforted to think of her in Heaven with Jesus. Finally, I could forgive myself.

'A few weeks later God really showed us his grace. I found that I was pregnant again and we now have another beautiful daughter.

'There have still been many problems since that night in January 1988. I have had to deal with many other things that stemmed from post-abortion trauma and some others that were caused by troubles further back, in my childhood.

'My main problems have been sexual ones, as well as low self-esteem and lack of self-confidence.

'I am slowly getting over these issues, but I know there must be thousands of other women still suffering in that darkness which I was once in. I do hope that the effects of what abortion can do can be brought to the attention of more women.'

SUGGESTED WORKSHOP/
DISCUSSION GROUP /PRO-LIFE SEMINAR.

1. Read Kay's story.

2. Each member of the group to think themselves into one of the people involved in Kay's story. Prayerfully think through your 'role' for about ten minutes, making notes if that will help to clarify your thoughts.

3. Discuss your findings in small groups/the group. Confess if this exercise has changed/formulated or confirmed your previous ideas, opinions, thoughts, on abortion on demand.

4. Bible work.
Read John 8:1-12; Luke 7:36-50; Mark 16:9; Isaiah 49:15, 16:5.

5. Discussion:
In the light of these readings, what would Jesus' attitude be to post-abortive women if he were here today?
Would you consider the abortion issue relevant to the Church 'agenda'? If NO, why not? If YES, what ought we to be doing, saying, in the name of Christ?
Would you consider Biblical 'sex education' to be relevant to the Church 'agenda'? If NO, why not? If YES, what ought we to be doing, saying, in the name of the Church on the subject?

6. Prayer.
For all those who have been led to believe that 'love' is physical gratification.
For those who have low self-esteem because of strings of broken relationships.
For those who have low self-esteem because of abortion.
For those who have contracted AIDS or other diseases as a result of their sexual activity.

For those struggling to maintain Christian standards for court-ship and relationships in spite of the current sexual laxity, in colleges, universities, away from home, etc.

For all M.P.s and especially those struggling to change the law and maintain Christian standards in Parliament.

For those children who have lost their Christian up-bringing because of upheaval in their childhood etc.

6. Discussion.

In the light of the earlier discussion on the Biblical stance, what can you do:

a) As individuals.

b) As a group.

c) As a church.

d) As a society.

Conclude with the blessing.

CHAPTER 10

THE RIPPLE EFFECT OF ABORTION

What of the ripple effect of abortion? Like a pebble thrown into a pool, abortion not only affects the immediate victims, the mother and child, but also partners, relatives, friends, carers, and many others who see what the consequences are.

A doctor's wife told her story:

'Ten years ago I was a happy contented housewife, with two children, Ros aged 17 and Dan, 12. They attended the local school and had a large group of friends who used to come home to ours for a meeting place. We lived in a lovely house, with a big kitchen and I always had biscuits and coffee on the go after school. Many of the other Mums had to go out to work, but fortunately, I was always able to be at home.

'One of our visitors was Kathy, an attractive girl a year younger than Ros. She was very promiscuous and I knew that she was "on the pill". Her conversation was dominated by talk of her boy-friend, Ken. He was older than she was.

'One day she discovered that Ken was going around with someone of his own age, a girl who was divorced. Kathy was heartbroken. She decided to stop taking the pill and then became pregnant. "If I'm expecting his child, he'll have to marry me," she reasoned.

'She told him the news and asked him to marry her, but his other girlfriend was also pregnant and he had promised to marry her.

'Kathy came from a loving, united, happy Catholic family. Instead of turning to her mother, she confided in a 35 year-old woman she had met at discos. This person had a young "toy boy" and must have seemed glamorous and wise to young Kathy.

' "You don't want to be stuck with a kid. Get rid of it!" was her advice. "You needn't tell your parents. Tell them you're staying a couple of nights at a friend's."

'Sadly, she took this advice and told her parents she would be with Ros at our home. I found out about this the day of the abortion and I was horrified. Of course it was too late! I could do nothing.

'To his credit, Ken did ring her parents and tell them that she was in hospital, not at ours. Her father telephoned the hospital in an attempt to save his grandchild's life, but it was all over.

'I was absolutely astounded at the incredible effect this sad episode had on me. I wept every day for three or four months for that little life, as if it had been my grandchild. I put the date in my Prayer Diary and I think of the little one who by now would have been at school. I pray for Kathy, with whom we have lost touch, since we moved house.

'Later, there was another girl who had an abortion in our social circle. This also made me very sad.

'What scares me, and I really mean scares me, is the lack of grandparental help. I suppose it is our more mobile society. People have to move around the country, to where their work is and do not turn to parents for help. My own grandparents were such a valuable part of my life as a child. Without the "extended family" there is less support for young marrieds, as well as for single girls who "get into trouble".'

IN MEMORY OF CHRISTINE

A visit to a young girl over twenty years ago changed the whole direction of Vince Crosby's life. A Catholic, he had joined the Society of St. Vincent de Paul as a junior in Manchester, then moved up into it's senior conference. After his National Service, Vince was in London and asked by his conference President to visit Christine, a young woman of around his own age who was suffering from depression. He went to the house, unexpected and unprepared, but after overcoming the father's initial coldness, became good friends with the family, who started going regularly to Mass again. Christine, however, still had bouts of depression. She was a graduate, destined for a future career in Corporate Law in the City. The family was very wealthy. Politically, socially, economically, they had everything.

Vince said: 'One evening, she confided to me that she had had an abortion, unknown to her parents, in a large London teaching hospital. She cried for a long time and seemed only to want to talk of the abortion. I was 29, unmarried and completely out of my depth. I tried to console her, with little success, then suggested that she confide in her parents and talk it out with them. She finally agreed to do this.

'Christine plucked up the courage to tell her parents. Her mother passed out and her father blew his top. I was caught up in the crossfire with no protection or experience of how to handle the situation.

'After reviving her mother, I made a cup of tea and spoke of the need to bring it all before God and think of Christine and the help and support she would need to come to terms with and be healed from the effects of the abortion.

'Two days later I went back to see how the family was coping. Christine said to me, "I killed my baby. How can God forgive me?" Three days later she died from an overdose of drugs, a cocktail of tranquillisers, barbiturates and alcohol.

'I went to the funeral and her mother came up to me and said, "Fight abortion." I promised, although I did not know how I was to do it. Her death affected me deeply. I felt responsible. I didn't go out and join a pro-life society. When abortion was mentioned I would become agitated. I felt violent towards people who argued in favour of abortion. Eventually I joined the Society for the Protection of the Unborn child' (SPUC).

Later Christine's mother wrote to Vince and said, 'I feel that you need to tell everyone about Christine ... From a material point of view we were far from poor and didn't need the S.V.P., even though Christine was depressed. But you persisted and became a very good friend, you brought God back into our home ... you must tell people ... the silence has to stop. I lost my only daughter through abortion and never saw my grandchild.'

Today Vince works tirelessly in the pro-life cause, writing, speaking, persuading. He says: 'I can never understand why I felt such hurt. I was devastated. I lost her and I resolved never to let it happen again, but I know that it does ... and that hurts because I can't reach those women. Whilst we can't turn the clock back and undo the abortion for any of these girls, we can show them that we care.'

A daughter's friend, a young girl committing suicide, and the hurt of abortion ripples through. So what of fathers, whose babies are aborted? Even a married man need not know under the present law that his wife is having an abortion. A woman can go into hospital for a 'scrape', and he will be no wiser. Is it fair that the father has no right to be told that his wife is pregnant, that his child is to be destroyed?

Arthur Shostak, an American sociologist, spent ten years studying the affect of abortion on fathers. He interviewed a thousand men before producing his book, *Men and Abortion: Lessons and Love*. He believes that this is an unrecognised trauma that men have to endure silently. The research was sparked off by the unexpected depths of grief and shock he felt when the child of himself and his former lover was aborted. This led him to ask if other men felt as he did.

For two reasons, it seems only fair that the father as well as the mother should have to sign 'the green form', sign their child's life away. On the one hand, it would save the child's life if the father refused to sign.

On the other hand, it could lower the rate of pregnancies and abortions, where the mother is left unsupported. Men might become more responsible if they had to make that crucial decision as well as the woman, who, in the early stages of pregnancy rarely feels well enough, physically or psychologically, to decide such a matter of life and death in a rational way. Too often, a man can walk away and leave a woman to cope on her own. On the other side of the coin, there are men like Arthur Shostak, men who care, who can do nothing to save their babies because it is the woman's right to chose. Genetically, the baby belongs to both of them. Legally, it has always been a father's right to provide for and protect his child. Abortion turns that all on its head. In the same way that surgically it is the only operation in which a doctor deliberately kills instead of heals, so legally, the father has no moral or statutory rights to protect his child.

Why is it that only abortion throws up this curious anomaly? How does abortion affect the medical profession and how has the emphasis changed to absorb it into the healing tradition of medicine?

Speaking to younger medical staff, I am amazed at the ignorance about abortion and its aftermath. For those who have grown up with a quarter of a century of abortion on demand, it seems the norm. Many have never thought it through, even Christians in the profession.

One ward sister, herself the mother of two children, told me:

'It's legal so there's not much we can do. When I was younger, it upset me a great deal. Nearly every woman said, just before going down to theatre, "Am I doing the right thing?"

'I felt that they should have a chat with someone, but my older senior sister said, "When they come to us they have had all the counselling. Two doctors have signed the form. Talking about it is done before that. Last minute fears are always there pre-op. The decision has been made. Our job is to get on with the operation and keep the schedule running smoothly. The rights or wrongs of it are nothing to do with us."

'As she was the senior, knew her job thoroughly and was kind to the patients, I too learned to make comforting sounds and make sure they were comfortable afterwards. If I leave gynaecology because of abortion, there may be more uncaring staff helping the women afterwards. And to be fair, they all seem to recover quickly and have a sense of relief.'

Of course they do! The immediate problem is solved, they're feeling physically better and, as most of our true stories show, that 'indescribable sense of loss' surfaces a few days after, when women are back home or back to work anyway.

Another Christian nurse went back to work after a three-year break and was sent straight into the gynaecological ward.

'I meet patients coming in for termination of pregnancy. At first I was very upset when I first met the issue of abortion. I was tempted to ask to be moved. After lots of prayer about it, I decided that it was better to stay and to pray for those involved.'

It is good that many pro-life nurses feel like this and are there to pray and also to let patients know where they can go for counselling if they need it, since it is rarely available in NHS hospitals.

In the Autumn of 1992, there was a television series on BBC 2 called DOCTORS TO BE, which followed six trainee doctors through various aspects of their course. I was not aware of the programme until I was told that the next one was to be on abortion. Since there has never been an abortion performed on TV (in spite of the fact that the act of conception is frequently portrayed, and most other operations have been covered to reassure patients), I watched this with interest. The viewer did not see the operation, only the faces of the watching trainees, and heard the 'talk-through', but there were comments after.

The amazing thing was that only two doctors chose to go! The G.P. is the first to see the patient when an abortion is requested, the first to sign 'the green form', yet seeing an abortion and knowing what it is all about is not obligatory in their training!

For the programme, there was one woman, Sarah Holdsworth, who said, 'I don't think I'll ever be able to do it ... it was the worse thing I've seen so far;' and one man, Nick Hollings, who were brave enough to watch. Nick commented that it made you realise that it was a human life being terminated. Sarah was upset at the tiny fully-formed arms, legs, etc., in the jar, which then had to be 'reassembled' by staff to make sure that all the pieces had come away from the womb. When asked if it had changed her mind about abortion, she said that it was a nasty process, but it was legal and someone had to do it. She said how upset she had been the first time a child had died and she had to tell the parents. Since then it had happened several times and she was learning to hide her own feelings and adopt a professional manner in these circumstances. She supposed it was the same for those performing abortions.

The surgeon who had performed the operation, Mr. David Paintin, said that no one liked it, but it had to be done. You did get used to it. Note that 'no one likes it'. But it has to be done. You can distance yourself from it, get used to it, do it clinically. Then the assumption, even in the medical profession, that if it's legal then it's alright.

For those who have always believed that medicine had a Hippocratic tradition of healing and saving life, it is difficult to come to terms with this operation, when the purpose is to destroy life. On the sad occasions when a hysterotomy has been performed and the child born live, it has to be left to die because that was the purpose of the operation, even though the same skilled team may be saving a premature baby on the same day in the intensive care unit because that is a wanted baby. How to reconcile this with the healing tradition? When a woman is pregnant the doctor has two patients. How have these double standards come about?

For a comprehensive study of this, read the Rev. Dr. Nigel de Cameron's book *The New Medicine* (published by Hodder & Stoughton 1992). Here a short explanation must suffice.

Up to a century ago, most patients trusted their doctor implicitly. Most were not as knowledgeable on medical matters, let alone other matters. Medical ethics was something that doctors practised as a daily routine, not something with which the Church challenged the profession, as today. The Church and medicine worked hand in hand. In each small area there would be the doctor and the parson/minister. Everyone would know everyone else, more or less. The parson would visit the sick, the bereaved and those with problems. The doctor would know who beat his wife, who could help another family in a crisis, as would the parson. It was mostly a team effort, even if the doctor was not heavily involved in the church. He had a good excuse not to attend anyway. His job also was seven days a week! Other doctors were devout churchgoers. Either way, socially, they would meet. The doctor's rich patients would be the church's generous benefactors.

In today's more mobile society we are no longer in small neighbourhood groups or villages, having to use the same doctor and the same church. We can choose doctors and churches. Our cars will take us to a more lively church or a more caring doctor. We watch television and read of things that go wrong medically. As a society, we do not necessarily trust the doctor any more than we go instinctively to the churchman for help. Why?

The school of Hippocratic thinking that produced the ancient Oath, taken by those entering the medical profession, was not only pagan, but very radical for its time. These physicians were in the minority, so why did their Oath catch on to embrace all faiths and none, and the medical profession worldwide?

Firstly, the Oath was the result of physicians' disgust with the practices of the day. Abortion and euthanasia were widespread in that ancient world, and these are the two negatives in the Oath which those ancient Greeks were striving to enforce. With all the passion and dedication of today's 'pro-life' movement, they carefully crafted the Oath.

'I will use treatment to help the sick according to my ability and judgment, but I will never use it to injure or wrong them.'

'I will not give a poison to anyone, though asked to do so, nor will I suggest such a plan. Similarly, I will not give a pessary to a woman to cause abortion. But in purity and in holiness I will guard my life and my art.'

Secondly, an oath has to be sworn to someone or something, and the all-embracing wording has been acceptable to all the major world religions. The oath was sworn by his 'God or gods' to do his best to heal his patients, respecting his teachers and profession. This has therefore a vertical and a horizontal aspect. To his God or gods above, to his teachers and fellow doctors on the earth, he promises to do his best for his patients. This lifts it above a narrow subjective view of the one-to-one doctor-patient relationship and involves the physician's whole life, his philosophy and the integrity of those who trained him and the rest of the medical profession.

The oath has a moral dimension too.

'Into whatever house I enter, I will do so to help the sick, keeping myself free from all intentional wrong-doing and harm, especially from fornication with woman or man, bond or free.'

'Whatever in the course of practice I see or hear (or even outside my practice in social intercourse) that ought never to be published abroad, I will not divulge, but consider such things to be holy secrets.'

From this we see that the Oath came from a pagan world with all the social problems we encounter: unfaithfulness, homosexuality, abuse, gossip. In spite of all this social deprivation, it was a moral oath, coming from the disgust with current practices. So after long centuries of Hippocratism, what has gone wrong that we have gone backwards to pagan practices, with abortion widespread and euthanasia a burning issue?

When the Hippocratic Oath was modernised in the 1948 Declaration of Geneva, the emphases were subtly shifted but seemed to pass unnoticed. It was in the aftermath of the Holocaust, when doctors had been answerable to the Nazi State alone and the words were updated, probably in all good faith, to:

'I solemnly pledge myself to consecrate my life to the service of humanity; I will give to my teachers the respect and the gratitude which is their due; I will practice my profession with conscience and dignity; the health of my patient will be my first consideration; I will respect the secrets which are confided to me; I will maintain by all means in my power the honour and the noble traditions of the medical profession; my colleagues will be my brothers; I will not permit considerations of religion, nationality, race, party politics or social standing to intervene between my duty and my patient; I will maintain the utmost respect for human life from the time of conception; even under threat I will not use my medical knowledge contrary to the laws of humanity; I make these promises solemnly, freely and upon my honour.'

Although this could be taken as a paraphrase of the original, it turned it into a secular oath, sworn before men.

In 1960, with the abortion debate and rate hotting up, the wording was again slightly changed:

'The utmost respect for human life from its conception' altered to 'the utmost respect for human life from its beginning', meant that those who would argue that conception was not the beginning, were able to abort with a clear conscience. Yet were they? If human life began when their so-called 'blob of jelly' reached and embedded in the womb, they were still destroying human life by the time the termination was performed, but the debate still rages as to when we become human! Today's technology and medical science has proved without doubt that conception is the moment when an amazing programme of development begins and each stage after that precedes another stage, continuing even after birth, as humans develop from babyhood to childhood, adolescence, adulthood, middle then old age.

It is extremely difficult for Christians to work in obstetrics and gynaecology these days, yet their compassion and witness is greatly needed there. The hurt and pain of abortion ripples through our world, through families, societies, creeds and professions, but especially through the medical profession.

Medical ethics have been made so much more complex by the frightening rate at which research and technology have expanded our powers of controlling the body and mind. These things are too complex for the lay mind, so it would be understandable for the Church to stand back and do nothing. Yet the great issues of life and death, the emotional and spiritual health of society is our business, as is violation against the works of the Creator. If those ancient Greek physicians could stand out against the pagan practices of their society and command a hearing, so should we, bearing in mind that we profess to have the power of the Creator of all life to help us.

SUGGESTED WORKSHOP/
DISCUSSION GROUP/ PRO-LIFE SEMINAR

1. Read a newspaper story involving medical ethics or give a short resume of the DOCTORS TO BE programme, or the changing nature of the Hippocratic Oath.

2. According to your age, sex or interests, think yourself into the role of one of the people in the story, or a member of the medical profession or of an abortion patient. Make notes on what you would do and how you think you would feel.

3. Discuss your findings. Note whether others who thought themselves into the same role had the same ideas. Confess if you have never thought through the subject before.

4. Bible Work: Read 2 Kings 8:12; Amos 1:13; Matthew 25:34-46.

5. Prayer:
For those in hospital having abortions.
For gynaecological staff who perform them.
For trainee doctors and nurses that they may be aware of the 'conscience clause' and refuse to do them.
For those who have to draft new laws, documents, etc., that they may realise that every word must be chosen carefully.
For all those who are troubled in conscience by the work they do.
For those who are standing up for their beliefs in difficult jobs.

6. Read Isaiah 49: 1,5,6. Discuss what you can do in the light of this:
   a) As individuals.
   b) As a group.
   c) As a Church.
   d) As a society.

Close with the blessing.

CHAPTER 11

WRITE THE DAY BEHIND YOU

If you have had an abortion and you cannot tell anyone, either because you have been ordered not to, or you are too ashamed to speak out about it, what can you do? Many women have found release in writing it all down. In one true story we read, 'Even writing it down has helped.'

Writing it down is a therapy, releasing the words, letting them go, just in the same way as confiding in somebody. Since starting post-abortion counselling and research, I have come across many poems, letters and stories, that women have written and hidden for years. A few have been printed or published. Some are great literature, others are not, but that doesn't matter. What matters is that the mother's feelings, grief, guilt, anxiety and plea for forgiveness, are all released and the pressure on them lessened.

Sharon, her real name because she wants everyone to know how awful abortion is, wrote this just after her termination, which devastated her. She was a nurse and thought it was all going to be over and done with and she could get on with her life and her career.

IF ONLY

Conceived, but unwanted,
Shall it cease to survive,
The life that grows,
Or go on, alone?

Where do I go
Will someone please help me
To seek advice
To decide what's right?

A decision is needed.
Please, someone, help me
Is it me or the child?
What to decide.

Is it a sacrilege to want   More out of life,
Not to be tied down,   To go out when I like?

A decision is needed ...   It's me or the child,
Please, someone, help me   What to decide.

The fourth of the eleventh,   Nineteen eighty-five,
The decision was made.   You did not survive.

I'm sorry, I'm sorry!   Words cannot express,
The feelings of emptiness   I now possess.

The all-famous saying,   'If I could go back',
Things would be different,   Be sure of that.

For your sake and mine,   I wish this could be,
If only, if only,   Someone had helped me.

On first reading that poem, I wondered why 'the fourth of the eleventh' and not 'the fourth of November', as most young people would have written today. The poet in me recognised that it would have read and scanned better, but the counsellor in me realised that Sharon had wrestled until the 'eleventh' hour for her and her child, with all the fears and indecision of any 'eleventh' hour or day or month, until that looming decision has to be made.

Like over half of the women who have terminations, Sharon went on to have another child within a year, to heal the hurting, even though under the same circumstances and with no-one extra to help or support her.

She wrote, when her son was a few months old, 'I felt so depressed and still do at times. I decided, when I came round from the anaesthetic, that this decision would never be made again in my life.

'I am now a single parent. My life has completely changed. I had to give up my work as a nurse. I never go out anywhere. My friends are all different. They still carry on going out with men and maintain exciting social lives. The only thing that is constant in my life is my son, whom I love very much. I have faced many difficulties and probably will face more in the future. But none of these will be as hard to come to terms with as the decision that I made to have an abortion.

'When I look at my son, at times I feel very sad to know that it was I who took a young life like his. I hope this letter will be of use to someone. I do not wish to be anonymous, although I am very ashamed of what I've done. If I can ever help anyone not to make the same decision, I will. I would say to any woman with an unplanned pregnancy, "If you cannot bring up your baby, please give him or her life. Please have the baby. There are plenty of childless people in this country who will love and care for this precious, individual gift." '

I wrote to suggest that Sharon might join a Mother & Toddler group and take up any hobbies she had previously enjoyed, to fill the long evenings when her baby was in bed.

She wrote, 'If only I had had someone to talk to, I know I would not have destroyed my child. People are still so against an unmarried mother. Other nurses and doctors gave me the cold shoulder. I had no offer of counselling before or after. When things like that happen to you, you do feel that you are the only one in the world this is happening to. If only women were aware of others who have been down this road.

'The fears were so real at the time. Already I was being judged, but when the baby came I'd be a single parent for ever, a social outcast, in general people not wanting to know you. This all sounds so silly now, but I experienced all these feelings of what might happen. In a way I took the coward's way out, but I am sure that if I had spoken to other women I would not have gone through with it. When I went to the doctor, he just sent me to the hospital. They seem to think it's routine.

'I am a very shy person and don't go out much. I will try and join a Group, as you suggest.'

Sharon wrote again after her son's first birthday, with a photograph. She had taken him to the zoo and he had loved it, then he had a Birthday tea with Sharon and an auntie and uncle.

'Did he make a mess! Being his party and being so young, I was not as strict as I normally am with his table manners. Needless to say, when the celebrations were at an end, he was briskly frog-marched into a waiting bath of bubbles. If you've seen the messy baby advertising baby wipes, that's what he looked like! I have not yet joined a Mother & Toddler Group. I could make many excuses, but it is that I am too shy to go by myself, yet I know that once I have made the effort I will be alright. One day I will wake up with the courage to get me there and I know it will be of great benefit to the baby as well. I did go through another time of depression recently, but went to the doctor and I feel fine now. The headaches have disappeared.

'I get a bit bored in the evenings, but recently I have started my old hobby of painting and I am also trying to teach myself calligraphy.'

Just a cameo there of a young Mum trying to do the best for her son, teaching table manners, obviously still ashamed of that earlier 'mistake' she made, trying to pluck up courage to get back into society. After an abortion, self confidence plummets down and even for Sharon, who was a nurse, some efforts to get out into the real world again seem just too much.

Not able to meet many people, spending hours alone with a baby with whom you can't discuss your thoughts, feelings or problems, writing it down, writing a poem, writing a letter, painting a picture, all helps to release something of Sharon back into that real world which still terrifies her because she thinks it will still be judgemental.

Many women keep a Diary or Journal and tell of how helpful it has been to 'Write the day behind you.' This of course is not only true of women after a termination of pregnancy. In many of life's traumas the Diary at the end of the day releases the tension. Then it's often possible to go to bed and sleep, rather than have all your anxious thoughts whirling around in the head. I found this particularly helpful when a close family member was involved in a serious road accident. Writing the day behind you, then committing the next one to the Lord's will, gives a measure of peace.

There are also books written by women after abortion. Noreen Riols story, already mentioned, was perhaps the first British one, long before post-abortion trauma was recognised as such. (Out of print in Britain, the French translation is still available, as we go to print.) Most after that have come from our American sisters, who have been into counselling and therapy long before we saw the need to release our thoughts and feelings. They are listed in the Bibliography at the end of this book. *One Day I'll See You* by Jennifer Doe is British and has helped many women.

Meg Matthews, who wrote the poems at the beginning of the book after going through the pain of the decision to abort or not to abort with a pregnant friend of hers, (another instance of the 'ripple effect') has also written *Quality Control*. She has worked with handicapped people, those visually and mentally handicapped and has done other voluntary social work.

QUALITY CONTROL

Seed met seed. They merged.
Life began.

Then anti-natal espionage
Decided on a Scan.

And they did tests
of every kind

And experimented,
Only to find

> They did not approve
> This fruit of love.
>
> Below the standard specified,
> Much better if it died.
>
> Recommended solution -
> Immediate abhortion.

The spelling mistake in the last line was a typing error, but a friend suggested that since abortion was so abhorrent, it ought to stay.

For many women, all that has relieved the secrecy, shame, guilt and grief of abortion have been words spilled onto pages, but sadly, hidden away from those other vulnerable women who should have been told the true facts.

In the same way as some mothers can come to terms with that 'indescribable sense of loss' by thinking of their child in heaven with the Lord, so others have found comfort in naming them, making them more a part of the family.   Many will recognise that their baby has an identity with God. Psalm 139:13-16 says:

> For you created my inmost being;
>   you knit me together in my mother's womb.
> I praise you because I am fearfully and wonderfully made;
>   your works are wonderful,
>   I know that full well.
> My frame was not hidden from you
>   when I was made in the secret place,
> When I was woven together in the depths of the earth,
>   your eyes saw my unformed body.
> All the days ordained for me
>   were written in your book
>   before one of them came to be.

How apt is this Psalm, written so many years ago, for the comfort of post-aborted women and for the inspiration of the pro-life movement!

However, it is also important that the child has an identity in the mind and heart of the mother, who often feels so guilty towards the baby, that whereas Jennifer Doe and countless others are comforted by the thought of meeting their unborn child in Heaven, others are terrified because they feel they need their babies' forgiveness. Some have written letters to the baby, asking for that forgiveness.

To mothers who have not undergone the stress of abortion, this may seem strange, but how else can forgiveness be sought? Some have hidden their letter away. Others have buried it in the grave of another loved family member. This also is not as strange as it may appear. In most bereavements, there is a grave, a tangible place where the earthly remains have been laid to rest, in consecrated ground. It can be a comfort for a grieving post-aborted mother to write out all her misgivings to her child and place it where she has said 'Goodbye' to another loved one. Some say that when they take flowers afterwards to that grave, they feel that they are also remembering and honouring their lost child.

CHAPTER 12

PHANTOM PREGNANCY

RITA'S STORY

Perhaps the most bizarre case I ever dealt with, or rather, failed to deal with, was one of phantom pregnancy.

I had heard of this phenomenon, but never experienced it in a counselling situation, except in the early stages, where it can be easier to deal with. With Rita, it lasted almost full-term. I never met her. Her live-in boyfriend contacted me because I was a LIFE counsellor.

Rita had just left him suddenly two weeks previously, after presumably going for an anti-natal appointment. The appointment was written on the calendar, just like all the previous ones. The spare room contained a brand new pram, cot, baby clothes and equipment.

When Rita failed to return from the hospital, Tom was worried. Later he rang a friend of hers, to enquire whether she had called there and been delayed. The friend confirmed that she was there, but refused to talk to him. When he persisted, he was told that it was best not to talk to her yet.

This situation lasted for about ten days, with Tom getting more and more desperate and confused, but other friends told him that this was probably Rita having pre-birth nerves and needing another woman's company. Tom was absolutely staggered to learn from the friend later, over the telephone, that Rita, although she desperately wanted to be, was not pregnant.

'Don't be ridiculous!' he answered. 'Of course she's pregnant. If it's anything I've done or said ... please ask her to see me. Let's talk it through. There must be a way out, whatever is wrong. We love each other.'

Rita adamantly refused to see him and her friend explained, as gently as possible, that it had been a 'phantom pregnancy'.

Tom thought he was going crazy. 'But she was huge ... there was milk in her breasts!'

When he recounted all this to me, I too wondered how the pretence/phantom condition had been kept up for so long.

'But what about the hospital appointments?' I asked.

'I checked them out. That was the first thing I did. I thought she wanted to split up with me for some unknown reason and didn't want me hanging around because it was my child. There were no hospital appointments. She knew which hospital and consultant some of her pregnant friends went to and she fabricated the appointments and wrote the next one down when she had "been" to the hospital for one. It's just too unbelievable for words. Yet what about the breast-milk?'

I explained that milk was produced as a result of hormonal procedures and that was feasible.

'But she was huge.'

'So are lots of people who eat well and let their muscles go,' I told him. He went on to confide that Rita had lots of psychological 'hang-ups' when he first knew her. She had been divorced, then on alcohol and drugs. She had once talked of a 'terrible secret', that she could confide to no-one, not even Tom. She did not have a criminal record. What was the terrible secret? Tom tried, through the friend, to get Rita to see me, or even another counsellor. She refused.

As the weeks went on and Tom and I kept in touch, all the signs pointed to Rita having had an abortion. She had been obsessed with the idea of starting a family first, although Tom had wanted marriage, not just cohabitation. He had gone along with her, feeling sure that once the baby arrived Rita would be more than glad to marry him. It was not to be. Rita refused to talk to him, to meet him or to resume the relationship. A few weeks later, her friend said she had returned to another part of the country where she had once lived. Tom visited the friend then and knew that it was true. The only message he had from Rita was that she was sorry. The friend confirmed that she was 'in a dreadful state'. Tom was left to dispose of the baby equipment and clothes.

Since Tom had himself been divorced ten years before and had been able to trust no-one until he met Rita, he needed counselling, too. We heard from him for a while afterwards and he said he would never feel able to make a relationship with a woman again.

As for Rita, she never again contacted any of her former friends. She told no-one where she was going.

Although I never had any factual evidence that this was a case of post-abortion trauma, Tom knew that she had never lost a baby or a child naturally. Neither did she have any medical reasons for not being able to have a baby. There had been children of the first marriage, but she lost custody because of her alcoholism and drug addiction. She had had treatment and was off these when she met Tom. In fact, her health seemed to have been restored as well as her psychological problems solved. However, it appears that these were only 'shelved'.

Cases of baby-snatching can be sometimes linked to the loss of a child, either by natural death or by abortion. Phantom pregnancy can also be attributed to such causes, or to the obsession to have a child. This over-anxiety can lead to body tensions which actually prevent easy conception. It can become a vicious circle. Maybe it was like that for Rita. We can only conjecture, but I will never forget Tom and will always feel a sadness for Rita and her lost hopes, remembering her in prayer.

WORKSHOP/GROUP WORK/SEMINAR GUIDE

1) Read Rita's story. According to your age, sex, orientation, think yourself into the character of either Rita, Tom, Rita's friend or a counsellor. Share how you felt with the group.

2) Bible work
Read Exodus 20:1-17 and Mark 12:29-31.

3) Discuss how secular forces have eroded people's happiness as well as their moral standards. If society will not listen to a Christian alternative, how can the Church begin by showing them that chastity, fidelity and a reverence for human life have been proved to be the only sensible safeguards for happiness and health and worth following even in non-Christian circles?

4) Pray for those in marriage crisis situations. (Leave time for members of the group to silently pray for any known to them personally.)
Pray for those unhappy after marriage break-up.
Pray for those dependant on alcohol or drugs following marriage/relationship break-up or abortion.
Pray for those with AIDS as a result of their sexual activity.
Pray for friends and confidantes of unhappy people.
Pray for counsellors, Christian and non-Christian.
Pray for Social workers and all others who seek to help.
Pray for the Church that she may be a light in dark lives.

5) Discuss what you can do to help the Ritas and Toms in your neighbourhood as
a) An individual
b) As a group member
c) As a Church
d) As a society.

PART 2

THE EFFECT OF ABORTION ON SOCIETY

CHAPTER 13

THE AFTERMATH OF THE ABORTION ACT

A quarter of a century ago, when the 1967 Abortion Act became law in this country, few realised that it would open the floodgates for abortion on demand. Today, with 95% of all abortions done for 'social' reasons, that has become reality. But should it have done?

In 1967 David Steel sponsored a Private Members Bill, which would protect a doctor from prosecution for performing an abortion, as long as two doctors signed a form to say that in their opinion, the continuation of the pregnancy would involve either:

a) Risk of life to the mother.

b) Risk of injury to the physical or mental health of the mother.

c) Risk to the physical and mental health of existing children, but only if these risks were *greater than if the pregnancy were terminated.*

d) If there was a substantial risk of the child being born seriously handicapped.

e) In emergency, to save the life of the mother.

f) In emergency to prevent grave permanent injury to the physical or mental health of the mother.

The Act contains a conscience clause allowing a doctor or nurse to opt out of performing abortions.

This Private Members Bill was given Government time to complete its passage through Parliament and came into force on April 28th 1968.

What it did not do was give a woman an automatic right to an abortion, or give a doctor a duty to carry out an abortion if a woman chooses to have one.

Twenty five years on, we know that is how it has been and is being interpreted. In those years four million unborn babies have been destroyed in England, Scotland and Wales. In a society where British justice has always stood for protecting the weak, especially those who cannot speak up for themselves, the aftermath of this parliamentary Act seems particularly incongruous. This is a flagrant display of discrimination, violence and violation of human rights: discrimination against the unborn, violence because nature cushions and protects the baby therefore abortion is a violent procedure; and violation of human rights, because in other circumstances an unborn baby does have human rights.

Today all seems to hinge on whether a child is 'wanted' or 'unwanted', although we know full well that an unwanted or unplanned pregnancy does not necessarily mean an unwanted child. Millions of women have been concerned at finding themselves pregnant when in financial or other dire straits, but have gone on to cope with the baby.

If a baby is wanted and the mother has a road accident which harms the child, compensation can be claimed through the courts. Likewise if a medical operation goes wrong, resulting in harm to the child which can be proven, then the unborn child has human rights and the full weight of the law to protect him or her. Legally, an unborn child can also claim an inheritance, if he/she has more right to it than a born relative. Today, in our 'civilised' country, people may feel apprehension walking the inner city streets after dark, flying across the world or riding the Underground in case of IRA bomb attacks, but the most dangerous place to be in this country and many other countries at this time is in the womb!

The reason for this is that the mother, who traditionally and naturally would have most right, incentive and instinctive urge to protect the child, now has the 'choice' to destroy that life within her.

When before has British justice depended on what your next of kin wants or chooses for you without your consent? In today's society, with the relaxation of the divorce laws and the debate on euthanasia, it seems to be going that way.

Yet pro-life counsellors know that most women do not want abortion. Some do decide completely on their own that their career, family, etc., must come first, but most women are pressurised into it by other people, as we have seen in our personal stories. Was this the intention of those who drew up and passed the Abortion Act?

As we saw in the case of the updating of the wording of the Hippocratic Oath, words are 'living'. They move and shift their meaning in the light of differing interpretations of their readers, either by the reader's character, orientation, upbringing, intellect or understanding of all the issues involved, or by the social climate and the 'language' or idiom of the day.

If we take the Act, or the clauses from it printed above, we can see how the emphases have subtly changed until we have in effect abortion on demand.

a) The risk to the life of the mother.
This has always been the exception to the rule for the surgeon. Always an abortion has been legal if it will save the life of the mother, if she and the father agree. In some families, the mother's life has been sacrificed in the past for the baby, but that has been the exception. Because the best medical attention was not available to poorer families, often in such circumstances the mother's life was deemed the most important, since there would invariably be other children to care for. In the light of today's medical science, there is rarely the need for abortion because the mother's life is in danger. Thankfully, medical research has made pregnancy safer than abortion.

b) The risk of injury to the physical or mental health of the mother.
This has been the clause where the widest interpretations have taken place. If in the early stages of pregnancy, with your hormones on a roller-coaster, morning sickness debilitating you for the first half of the morning, worried because of finance, accommodation, relationship difficulties, your job or education at stake, you go to a doctor and spill this all out, it can be defined as injury to your physical and mental health.

Coupled with c), *the risk to the physical or mental health of your existing children*, the arguments to abort are reinforced. If you have this child your youngest child will feel 'left out', your teenage daughter can no longer expect you to chauffeur her and her friends around and it's not safe to walk alone at night, you will no longer be able to afford their school holidays you promised, or the family holiday or ... so the arguments go on ... round and round in your head, until you believe them yourself ... but only because you have the choice! Only because women expect a better standard of living. Their right to a nice home, necessities like car, television, telephone, holidays, which used to be termed 'luxuries', can supersede the right of their children to be born, but again, only because the Abortion Act gave them that right, albeit obliquely.

d) accounts for most of the 5% of abortions that are not performed for the social reasons listed above. If there is a substantial risk of the child being born seriously handicapped, the mother has a 'choice'. The problem is that the choice is not a free choice, but seems more a case of succumbing to pressure, often unfair because it plays on her love for and desire for the future wellbeing of her child. When my sister-in-law was pregnant at 42 years old she was asked five times if she wanted a termination. At no point had she enquired about the possibility or requested one! For a generation who have been brought up to think that the doctor knows best, this is an unwanted pressure when a woman is at her most vulnerable both physically and mentally. Many older women confide that they are made to feel ashamed that they have become pregnant.

How many women know that the amniocentesis test, where a sample of the amniotic fluid is drawn off and tested for possible handicap, itself carries a 1% chance of miscarriage occurring as a result of the procedure? Today a three-in-one test is now routine for all pregnant women, and this can confirm the possibility of Down's Syndrome in the child. Again this puts undue strain and worry on the mother for the duration of the pregnancy. None of these tests can be forced on a woman, but their very existence, while supposedly for the good of the child, mostly result in the pressure to abort. The rights of handicapped people to exist in our society is a whole other subject, but for the handicapped unborn child the danger and threat to life is immense.

In 1990, The Human Fertilisation and Embryology Act, amended the 1967 Act by inserting a 24 week limit for abortion on grounds a, b, and c. It also introduces a new ground, for 'grave, permanent injury to the physical or mental health of the pregnant woman'. Is this to be taken as literally and loosely as we have seen before? Already we have heard wild statements that stretch marks could be truthfully defined as 'permanent injury'!

This category has no time limit, therefore abortions can be performed up to birth. No time limit was also introduced for risk of handicapped babies, clause (d) above. In these instances the Infant Life (Preservation) Act, of 1929 does not apply and no doctor can be prosecuted under it. (This Act gave protection after 28 weeks of pregnancy, when a child was deemed 'capable of being born alive'.) We have to bear in mind that there were no intensive care units or technology to help and a 28 week or over baby had to survive unaided by medical science. Today babies are capable of being born alive at much earlier dates with the help of modern invention. For those of us engaged in post abortion counselling, the key words are, in the 1967 Act, after (c), GREATER THAN IF THE PREGNANCY WERE TERMINATED (my capital letters).

In the light of the personal stories here recorded, are the 'social' reasons or risks greater than the results of abortion? Since post-abortion trauma is not yet officially recognised in this country and was unheard of in 1967, the intention of the Act then surely was a different thing altogether. Now we know the after effects of abortion. Women have told us and are telling us. Is not post-abortion trauma much more serious and devastating than any of the projected outcomes of the 'social' causes?

Dr. Vincent M. Rue, Ph.D., the American psychiatrist, started studying the effects of abortion when he traced many of his clients problems back to an earlier termination. It took twelve years for him to gain public acknowledgement of his findings, but eventually, in 1987, the American Psychiatric Association officially recognised Post Abortion Syndrome (PAS) as a PTSD, that is, a post-traumatic stress disorder. Vincent Rue, who also treated Vietnam war victims, has put PAS on a par with their psychological trauma. In fact, seeing these traumatised women exhibiting the same symptoms and behaviour as men returning from Vietnam, caused him to begin his research.

Dr. Rue says, contrary to most doctors, that spontaneous recovery is not characteristic after abortion. A large study covering the whole of Denmark found that women were much more likely after abortion to need hospital treatment for their psychological needs, than for the birth of their babies! This leads us to ask just how much is spent on drugs and treatment for women with 'depression', after an abortion. We know that the NHS., the largest dispenser of drugs in this country, spends a colossal amount on treatment for mental ill-health. Because PAS often surfaces so long after the abortion, how often is it attributed to that cause in the doctor's records? Would a full study of all those women on tranquillisers, sleeping pills, anti-depressants, etc., give us some of the answers if coupled with the abortion records?

And what of other drugs, self prescribed? In a Scottish study of 1,008 women with drinking problems, 23.6% (238), reported previous obstetric problems, 110 of these being pregnancy termination by induced abortion. Spontaneous abortions, (miscarriages), accounted for a further 94. Alcohol is frequently used to deaden the pain of death or loss, as we well know. The loss to industry, commerce and the family wellbeing as a result of alcoholism is also well known. How much does abortion cost us in real terms, both monetary and pyschologically? We need much more research, but initially, we need PAS recognised in Britain by the medical profession at large and accepted by the British Medical Association (BMA) and the Royal College of General Practitioners. For the five years since America officially recognised PAS, abortion figures that we know of (and back-street abortions still do occur, as in Suzie's case in Chapter 6, so there could be more), give an average of over 180,000 legal terminations a year in England, Scotland and Wales. In 1990 the figure was 186,912. Even given that over half of these will have another baby within a year, there are still a lot of women recently aborted, who need Post Abortion counselling before the problem compounds into more serious consequences.

Dr. Rue has assessed women as acutely stressed when such stress surfaces within six months of the abortion and last less than six months, and chronically stressed when it lasts longer than six months. Delayed reaction often occurs, where a woman has blotted out the experience, and typically this happens seven or eight years afterwards. Although this blotting out process occurs, yet the woman's behaviour is continually affected by her feelings of emptiness, loss, guilt and lack of self-esteem, which she refuses to bring out into the open and seek help to deal with. She will have had to cope with strong feelings of denial, trying to convince herself that this trauma she is going through is not associated with her decision to abort.

Dr. Rue says that the abortion experience, i.e. the intentional destruction of one's unborn child, is sufficiently traumatic and beyond the range of usual human experience, so as to cause significant feelings of re-experience, avoidance and impacted grieving. Sometimes she may seek help for one problem without revealing her termination. She can go to a doctor or a counsellor for: depression, suicidal tendencies, a pre-occupation with death or dying, (often believing herself terminally ill), broken relationships, anger, drug/alcohol abuse, sexual problems, phobias, unnatural fear for her existing children, infertility, eating disorders like anorexia or bulimia, sleeplessness, psychosomatic physical pain, concentration problems, phantom pregnancy or self-punishment.

These are all symptoms of post-aborted women, but how often are they linked with abortion? They can also be caused by other stressors, particularly in women who have been physically or sexually abused. Not every woman with such problems will be an aborted woman, but the links could well be investigated.

In the USA, 1800 out of 4,000 women calling Suicide Anonymous (a line like our Samaritans), in a 35-month period, had had an abortion or abortions. (Research: Meta Uchtman, Suicide Anonymous, Ohio.) (N.B. The suicide rate in pregnant women is almost nil. After giving birth it goes up to the national average. After abortion it escalates dramatically, according to an Irish study, covering 4,000 deliveries over ten years. Yet abortions are performed for the mental health of the mother!) If a woman becomes pregnant again quickly, this may give her obsessional fears about the baby's well-being, fear of internal examinations, of hospitals, gynaecological staff, in fact anything that will remind her of her abortion. This could trigger off again the nightmares, flashbacks to the abortion experience, the guilt and the impacted grief. For most women the second child will be a healing experience, but for others it can only reinforce just what it meant when the first pregnancy was terminated, just what the abortion did.

Because of all this, many women may also experience difficult labours when they do start a family.

The longer a woman tries to cope with the post-abortion experience alone, the worse it gets. Anniversaries are always a problem. She knows if her child would have been a year or ten or twenty-one. She may have a fixation of a child in the family or social circle of the same age. She may criticize the parents' dealings with the child. Alternately, she may not be able to relate to children or young people at all and cause problems in the family. If no-one knows the reason she ignores their child or children, this can further isolate her.

Susan Stanford, another American psychologist, who herself had an abortion in order to carry on with her career, worked with Dr. Rue. She was drawn to the research because of the unexpected feelings she had experienced. Her book, *Will I Cry Tomorrow*, tells of her own journey out of post-abortion syndrome and how

God finally healed her and gave her the 'tool' with which to heal other women.

Susan herself was healed when she changed places and sat in the client's chair. She was led gently back into her own abortion experience, by a Christian counsellor. With closed eyes, she was asked to go back in her memory to the time of her abortion. She was led to see Jesus holding her baby safely in his arms. She had always thought of her child as a boy. She 'saw' him in a blue blanket. As the tears flowed, Susan felt an inner healing. She named him, acknowledging him at that moment as a person, a member of the family.

After this, she realised that she needed to match her training and knowledge in psychological diagnosis and counselling, with her Christian experience. How was she to do this, when most of her clients were non-Christian?

She prayed that somehow she could 'mix' her training, her experience and her faith to find the right 'recipe' for other women who were hurting. She continued to pray and work on this for a long time, going to all the healing and psychological conferences she could.

Even so, the first time she tried out her new technique, she felt as inadequate as any new counsellor and had to pray her way through. After that, she soon came to realise that even if most women are not professing Christians, most have a deep belief in a Creator God. Many have a background belief in Jesus, from Sunday School or day school stories, yet do not have a personal relationship with him. In many cases she was able to draw out some sort of belief. Some women were ready to 'try anything' and had to be skilfully led back to the abortion room. Their knowledge of God as a God of love, of Jesus as one who forgives and loves, was used, as they were asked to imagine him in that room with them during and after the abortion. Many people have a vague belief that 'God is everywhere', although they seem to manage without acknowledging that he is there. If he was there, at the abortion, after the baby was taken from the mother, what would he do? If God was the Creator, if he had made this little life, what would he do with it now? Susan was able to lead other women to see their babies taken care of by God, taken into the arms of Jesus.

When 'healing memory' sessions such as this are carried through with much prayer for the Holy Spirit's guidance, God can heal. However it needs a skilled counsellor to know just when the woman gets to this point. It is easier to reach this with the Christian woman, who knows deep down within herself that she is forgiven because the love of God as displayed by Jesus on the Cross is bigger than her sin. Yet that abortion room, because secret from most of her associates and fellow-church members, is seen by her to be a place of evil where she has never imagined God to be, except perhaps as a condemning judge. Once she is led to see Jesus there, with all his love and forgiveness offered to her, as he takes her child into his care, there is healing.

But even such spiritual healing does not automatically deal with all the other problems the aborted woman has. It will still be a long process of one step forward and two back, as with prayer and love and skilful counselling she has to work through and seek healing for her relationships, learns to forgive herself and to see herself as a child of God, with a self-confidence and esteem to match.

David Seamans, at the end of his book, *Healing Memories*, says 'Following the crisis of memory healing, the very important process of relearning and reprogramming needs to take place.' The aborted woman will need to learn new perceptions and new ways of relating to God as well as to others, once she is cleansed from her destructive memories and behaviour.

It is impossible for counsellors in the post-abortion field to set any kind of a pace or timescale for healing. The damage has been done over years, mostly, and people are all very different.

Some counsellors believe that there is no need to work up to certain points or stages, but that just by being there, in time, it will all be confided and each area can be dealt with as it arises. For Susan Stanford, who was in the business of psychology, if possible the spiritual healing had to come first with her clients, although she admits that it is always governed by just where the client is at the time. After that, Susan felt that the rest came more easily. For those who have very little or no Christian comprehension, which is often the case with today's younger women, the Christian counsellor has to tread a delicate and often long path.

Counsellors need to have thorough training and the pro-life organisations provide that for their counsellors. There are national networks of pro-life work and it should be a simple matter for anyone to put a post-aborted woman in touch with the help she so desperately needs.

God says through the prophet Hosea: 'My people are destroyed through lack of knowledge' (Hosea 4:6.) Never more so than in the field of abortion worldwide!

CHAPTER 14

THE GENERAL EFFECT OF MASS ABORTION

As we have seen, there are many repercussions for a society with a 25 year history of mass abortion. Just six of the obvious ones will be touched on here.

1. The psychological aftermath which has been well-documented in Part 1.

Suffice to say that the cost to the nation in terms of continuing medical attention, either for depression or mental disturbance must far exceed the cost of research which should then without a doubt lead to proper pre- and post-abortion counselling. There is also a cost in terms of careers abandoned, broken relationships, extra sick leave for those dependent on alcohol or drugs, often leading to unemployment benefit, housing benefit and Social Services involvement. The entire 'bill' for the aftermath of abortion cannot be envisaged. That is all extra to the lives ruined by this trauma. Can we afford it?

It would be unfair to say that nothing is being done. A paper entitled, 'Sequelae of induced abortion', presented at a 3-day symposium on abortion says: Although a substantial amount of work has been published on the sequelae of induced abortion, it is generally agreed that much research so far has been faulty in method and inadequate in scope... (Ciba Foundation Symposium. 1985 vol.115. publ. Pitman, London). 1,509 G.P.s and 795 gynaecologists in England, Scotland and Wales are taking part in a long term controlled study on abortion's after effects. Their findings are awaited eagerly. Interim results are listed below.

2. The physical aftermath

Of 6,105 patients studied, results show that in the first 3 weeks after the abortion 10% returned to the doctor with a complication arising. 2.1% of these were major complications and 2.4% psychological. Two patients were admitted to a psychiatric hospital. (Ciba Foundation Symposium vol 115, pp 67-82). For many patients of course complications arise later. Instruments which are used in abortion can in some cases perforate the womb and then damage loops of bowel lying adjacent to the uterus. When the surgeon suspects that he has damaged the uterus, he performs a laparotomy, an exploratory operation on the abdomen, to check the bowel and repair any damage. The risk of this complication varies according to the state of pregnancy.

A common figure for abortions taking place in the first trimester, i.e. the first 13 weeks, is quoted at between 1 and 3 perforations per 1,000 abortions. In one study of 6,408 first trimester abortions, the rate was 1.3 per 1,000, but 706 of these patients were sterilised at the same time. When this was done another twelve were discovered to have unsuspected perforations, as well as two already recognised, giving a rate of 19.8 per 1,000 terminations. This shows how inadequate are the statistics we have at our disposal for any accurate knowledge of the rate of perforation. Second trimester (13-26 weeks) abortions carry a higher rate, but note that since these are carried out under ultrasound control, the surgeon can clearly see what is happening, as the child is dissected. There is a risk of miscarriage for subsequent pregnancies after abortion, especially in younger women.

This is due to the cervix, the neck of the womb, having to be unnaturally stretched to allow the surgeon's instruments to pass through. The cervix, a powerful muscle which normally seals the baby firm inside the womb, can then lose its elasticity, causing a miscarriage. A study from Yugoslavia found a 10.7% rate of spontaneous miscarriage among girls who had had an abortion at 14-16 years old, compared with 5.5% of older adolescents. 24% of the youngest, delivered a premature baby, compared with

10.3% of girls of the same age who had not had a previous abortion. (Jugoslavenska Ginekologija i Perinatologija 1986 Vol 26 pp 49-52.)

Since today many women have a number of sexual partners, we have seen a rise in Clamydia, an organism which infects the cervix. The problem is that it often causes no symptoms, therefore many women are unaware that they are infected. Most studies now report that between 10 and 25% of women requesting abortion carry this infection. Some isolated studies have put the figure as high as 43%. The carriage rates for Clamydia is much higher in younger women. In Scandinavia these were 16.8% for women up to 19, 11.5% for 20-24 year olds, 7.4% for those 25-29 years and 3.2% for the 30+ age group, giving an overall average of 9.3% . (Acta Obstetrica et Gynecologica Scandinavica 1988 vol 67, pp 525-529).

The problem occurs when an abortion is performed because, as the instruments are passed into the womb, they carry the organisms from the cervix into the womb itself. There is an ideal environment for them to grow in the raw tissue and blood clot left behind after the operation. The infection is thus set up and can spread to the fallopian tubes. This is called Pelvic Inflammatory Disease.

A study carried out in a day care abortion clinic in Liverpool found Clamydia in 11% of abortion patients. 18% had mycoplasmal infection and another 18% other vaginal infections. (Some women had several infections, so these percentages cannot be added together.) At the first visit after the abortion, 4% had symptoms of pelvic inflammatory disease and 8% symptoms of less serious infection. So in 12% of these women the infection had spread from the cervix to the tubes. They all required urgent chemotherapy. After this, a further 8% developed symptoms and were treated by their own doctors. This gave a 20% figure of post-abortion infection. It is interesting to note that 35% of these had had 4 or more sexual partners. Only 12% of those who did not develop post-abortion infection had had 4 or more partners.

To collate other studies, research shows that between 10 and

40% of women presenting for abortion have Clamydia infection. And of these 10-25% will develop post abortion pelvic infection. That means that between 1 and 10% of all women having an abortion will develop serious pelvic infection afterwards. In the USA many abortion clinics now test and treat for genital infections before the abortion, but this is not done in the U.K.

3. The elimination of handicapped babies is another result of abortion.

In today's climate of advanced technology, where more and more handicapped people are being helped to live fuller and more rewarding lives, the moral climate is such that society deems them of little worth. Pre-natal screening is done to prevent handicap we are told. It's results so far have been to prevent handicapped children being born. Obviously we could stamp out any disease if we killed off all those affected with it! We could stamp out murder if we screened for the most likely and killed all potential murderers.

Mostly, 'potential' handicap is the only result we get from pre-natal screening. The degree of handicap is usually not known and many women after months of worry have gone on to produce perfectly healthy babies. Most of the older women who complain that they are made to feel ashamed of being pregnant, produce healthy children. All we know is that the risk of handicap is greater in older women. Does that justify a 42-year-old being asked 5 times if she wants an abortion?

For women who do have abortions because they are expecting a handicapped child, there is a support group, SAFTA (Support after Termination for Abnormality). This group produces a helpful leaflet covering some of the important aspects of making a decision to abort and the practical and physical requirements afterwards. The last paragraph in this leaflet deals with the questions that arise as to any future pregnancies and the questions that need to be asked, which are often not thought of when the distressing operation takes place.

The whole question of the worth that society today gives to

disabled people is a whole other subject. Suffice to remind readers of two children born in the same hospital on the same day and delivered by the same doctor. One was a strong, healthy boy, lustily making his entrance heard. The other was a severely handicapped girl. One grew up to lead his nation. The other had a happy, quiet existence at home in a country village. She was a willing worker in and around the home and finally nursed her mother loyally through terminal illness. The doctor paid tribute to the worth of her life. The boy he delivered that same day was Adolf Hitler.

4. More sexual activity outside marriage seems to have been another after effect of the Abortion Act.

While abortion is not meant to be used as birth control or population control, trends throughout the world point us to the conclusion that this is often so. The 'risk' factor of a permanent reminder or result of sexual activity was taken from many people's minds after abortion was legalised. If a woman became pregnant, there was now a way out, and more people were prepared to take the risk of pre-marital or extra-marital sexual activity. However, we know that people who equate sex with 'love', with no loyalty or responsibility attached, find a hollow satisfaction. There may be more sexual activity but there is less happiness or real love between couples who have no other qualities of commitment or longterm loyalty between them. Today the rate of marriage and relationship breakup causes untold unhappiness.

In the above section on Clamydia just one medical aspect of the result of such sexual activity is shown. The slogan 'SAFE SEX' has deluded a growing generation into believing that only 'protection' is needed. The times that protection fails, the high risk of sexually-transmitted diseases, some of them life-threatening, like AIDS, seems to have been forgotten in the light of those two magic words, 'SAFE SEX'. If it worked, the teen pregnancy as well as the abortion rate would dramatically drop.

Abortion has given the green light for people to have more than one sexual partner. It has been pointed out that if you have slept with six people who have slept with six people who have slept with six people etc. ... who knows what has been passed on. Just work out the huge numbers to the above hypotheses on the same basis as the old 'chain letter' numbers are calculated. Over a period of the years of your sexually active life, you could have been affected or infected by a quarter of the world!

Another offshoot of this 'safe sex' attitude is the way in which it has been promoted in schools and amongst young people, assuming that all young people are sexually active. How many are because they think they 'ought to be' and there's something wrong with them if they are not? When lots of youngsters should be concentrating on their exams or other normal adolescent activities, many of them are going through emotional upheaval because of their too early relationships with the opposite sex. At rock bottom, ask any young person and he or she will admit that they would prefer to marry someone who had not already slept with someone else.

When is the Church going to shout from the rooftops that chastity is not only desirable for Christian couples, but absolutely necessary for all couples, for physical as well as mental health reasons. Jealousy is still one of the commonest causes of marriage breakup and some jealousies result from past relationships as much as present ones. The 1967 Abortion Act has helped to promote sexual laxity.

5. Elimination of child abuse a myth.
'Every child a wanted child' was another 1967 slogan. It was stressed that unwanted and abused children would be a thing of the past. The reality is, as we all know, that abuse has in fact risen. Is it that children are regarded as of so little worth, since they can be disposed of before birth, that they are deemed of no importance after? Maybe that is too sweeping a statement.

Equally it may be that the sexual laxity mentioned above has caused more marriage breakup, more co-habitation and more changing of partners. Other people's children are not always accepted, cherished and loved as are one's own. While there are millions of wonderfully caring step-parents and second partners in our society, there are also live-in boyfriends and girlfriends who do not care how they treat their partner's children of a former relationship. The sad facts are that now that every child could be a wanted child, not every child is. On the other side of the coin, many children who have been destroyed in the womb would have been loved and cherished and wanted.

6. Smaller families.

Has abortion on demand created our families of 2.4 children, or is that due to contraception or to financial strictures? While it is arguable as to whether bigger families are happier families, valuable lessons of 'give and take' are learned in the home in a larger family unit. Some of today's '2.4' children seem to 'have everything', and grow up with the idea that society owes them a living. Others of course grow up to be responsible members of society, but size of families is another aspect of the contraceptive and abortion revolution being discussed by sociologists.

As we have seen, abortion has ripple effects across society and medicine, as well as medical, psychological and ripple effects for individuals and families. When we go on to look at other countries in chapter 17, we shall also see where it has been used for birth control and population control. Many nations, especially former Communist states, are beginning to look at abortion in a new light. So should we.

SUGGESTIONS FOR WORKSHOP/
GROUP WORK/PRO-LIFE SEMINAR.

1. Consider the 1967 Abortion Act. Divide the group into two. Ask one to look at it from a totally secular standpoint, and discuss what they consider to be the advantages and disadvantages since 1967. Ask the other group to discuss it from a Christian viewpoint. Bring the two groups together to give their findings.

2. Bible work:
Read Genesis 33:5; Psalm 127; and Psalm 128.

3. Discuss the picture of life depicted in these readings. Compare it with today's attitude towards family life, generally speaking. Discuss whether in your opinion, larger families are happier families. Ask if the Church as you know it, promotes a Biblical view of family life.

4. Pray for the victims of abortion. Pray for families torn apart by physical or sexual abuse. Pray for those grieving for aborted children. Pray for researchers, those involved in medical ethics today. Pray for the Church that she may be a witness to the strength of the family and its effect on national life.

5. Discuss how to strengthen and support family life in Britain as:
    a) an individual
    b) as a group
    c) as a Church
    d) as a society.

Close with the blessing.

CHAPTER 15

THE METHODS OF ABORTION, PARTICULARLY RU 486.

At the moment there are seven methods of abortion. The method used depends on the gestational age of the child, that is, in which trimester the termination is performed. In some cases more than one method has to be used.

The methods are as follows and are given, not because the purpose of this book is to dwell on the violence or horror of abortion, but because one of them will be having far-reaching effects on post-abortion trauma in the future.

1) Vacuum Aspiration is the suction method of abortion, performed in the first trimester, under anaesthetic. The neck of the womb, the cervix, is opened and the 'products of conception' sucked through a tube into a jar, in pieces. 85% of abortions in England and Wales are performed like this, in the first thirteen weeks of pregnancy.

Some NHS hospitals are now only doing abortions this way. For later ones private abortion clinics have to be sought. This in turn pushes the mother to make a swift, often regretted decision, because she does not have £400 or so for private fees.

2) Dilation and Curettage (D & C), has been almost replaced by the suction method. Here the womb is 'scraped', with a curette, destroying and removing the foetus, but parts could be left, causing infection and often future infertility. (Specialists cite abortion as a major cause of infertility.)

3) Dilation and Evacuation (D & E) is used with later pregnancies.

Small forceps are used instead of a curette, because the foetus will be larger.

4) For bigger babies, prostaglandins are used to induce premature labour. This does not need a surgical operation, since prostaglandins are injected or given as pessaries to bring on the labour, which is usually intense and lasts approximately 8-22 hours. Many late abortions are performed this way. Because the child can be large enough to live for a short time after birth, which was distressing for mother and staff, poison is often added to the water in the womb to ensure a dead child. Obviously this does mean a more difficult birth.

5) Hysterotomy is now rarely used except in very late abortions. It is almost the same as a Caesarean section, the operation used in difficult deliveries. The difference is that this child will not be rushed to the intensive care unit and kept alive. Now that the law has been changed to abortion for handicapped babies up to birth, any parents changing their mind at a later stage will need this method.

6) Post-coital contraception, the so-called 'morning after pill', is more and more often prescribed within 72 hours of unprotected pregnancy. Although termed 'contraception', conception may have occurred, therefore it is an abortifacient in intent. Two high dosage tablets containing the oral contraceptives levonorgestrel (250 micrograms), ethinyloestradiol (50 micrograms), brand names Ovran and Schering PC4, are taken within the first 72 hours of intercourse, then a further two tablets 12 hours later. Risks to long-term health are as follows:

A small risk of thrombo-embolic and cardiovascular complications, increasing with age, smoking or obesity.

A greater risk if you have a family history of diabetes or hypertension. Textbooks on drugs also caution on this method for women with migraines, epilepsy, depression, asthma, varicose veins or who wear contact lenses!

7) The latest method of abortion is the abortion pill RU486. This is the one of greatest concern in the context of post-abortion trauma, since it is still fairly new, has not been thoroughly tested in many both pro-life and pro-abortion opinions and yet is being increasingly adopted by various health authorities in this country and throughout the world. The first stories are coming in and they do not make pleasant reading.

Before RU486 was licensed over here, in July 1991, 100,000 French women underwent these chemical abortions. RU486, or mifegyne, or mifepristone, to give it all its names, is used in conjunction with prostaglandins to bring about an end to the pregnancy. It was first formulated by the French-based drug company Roussel Uclaf in 1980 and was the cause of intense controversy. It was licensed, then banned, then licensed again in France, when it was advocated a 'safe' method, but pro-life and other medical opinions differ on that issue. The first licensing was based, as far as one can discover, on tests only by the manufacturing company itself, and that company had poured a great deal of money into the pill's formulation, production and promotion.

Claude Evin, French Health minister is said to have called it 'the moral property of women', when he re-issued the licence, the withdrawal of which was attributed to pro-life pressure, not safety. Yet, the company itself advises that the following facilities should be available where the drug is used:

An ultrasound scanner.
Laboratory facilities for assessing blood samples.
Adequate facilities for administering prostaglandins.
Adequate nursing and counselling staff.
Narcotic pain killers.
Cardiovascular monitoring equipment.
Emergency resuscitation medication and equipment.
Emergency theatre facilities.
(Roussel Uclaf's booklet on RU486, p.10, *Necessary Facilities*).

These are not stipulated by law, yet recommended by the manufacturer! Many abortion clinics do not have all these facilities. So how can this new method, hailed as a gift to women, be termed as safe as other methods? It has also been hailed as preferable to surgical abortion, according to a National Opinion Poll survey (DOCTOR, January 9th 1992. 'Clinics set pace for abortion pill,' pp.44-45.), so have women been told the true facts?

The pill, which is a powerful cocktail of drugs, was tested on animals for only 18 months. Early trials gave a 54%-90% success rate compared with other methods. The trials continued, with other companies also researching similar compounds of abortifacients. Roussel Uclaf rushed theirs onto the market.

It works, put in simple terms, by starving the baby of essential nutrients and making its environment hostile.

As early as 1968, Professor R. V. Short, of the Department of Veterinary Clinical Studies at Cambridge University said, 'If we are to control human population one of the things we need to control is the human corpus luteum' (*Foetal Autonomy Ciba Foundation Symposium*, P. 6. published by J. A. Churchill, Ltd., 1969).

Mifepristone works by attacking the function of the corpus luteum, the follicle which, after ovulation, is emptied, but continues to secrete progesterone, to prepare the womb for pregnancy. This goes on for the first seven weeks of pregnancy, the period when RU486 is deadly effective. Also in 1969, the International Population Union Conference on the scientific Study of Population was involved in a project to 'search for a monthly oral preparation which would destroy the corpus luteum whether or not fertilisation had taken place' (International Population Union Conference Report, London, 1969 p. 1355).

So much for Population control, but what about the pregnant victim? This is not a simple DIY pill! It can involve up to 4 visits to a clinic and can last up to 12 days. Hardly painless or confidential either! But for the potential problem of post-abortion trauma, the most horrendous part is that some women will abort at home, probably alone, and could have to dispose of their 'products of conception' themselves. In our modern, sophisticated society, as well as reverting to pagan medical ethics, we also seem to be reverting to the horrors of back-street abortion.

This complicated procedure has several stages:

1) The woman has to be counselled and advised. Her medical history has to be looked at. This method is not advisable if there are indications of: asthma, cardio-vascular disease, epilepsy, kidney disease, liver disorder, allergies, adrenaline deficiency, pulmonary disorders, suspected ectopic pregnancy, and moderate to heavy smoking. When asked to define 'moderate' and 'heavy' smoking, 'moderate' was assessed at ten cigarettes a day and 'heavy' as twenty. Many women smoking ten to twenty cigarettes a day would not term themselves 'heavy' smokers. Will they give the right answers and be aware of the dangers? Obviously the above list eliminates some women. They will also need to be between 18 and 34 and be under 9 weeks pregnant. This cuts out many more.

Next a pelvic examination, an ultrasound scan, urinary and blood samples are needed to confirm the pregnancy and determine the gestational age of the baby.

2) 600 mg of mifepristone is given in 3 tablets, either at the same time as the counselling session or in a subsequent visit. (N.B. In France women are asked to go home for 24 hours to make sure about their decision. Here in the U.K. the pills are given usually at the first visit.) If vomiting occurs, during the next two hours when the woman is being monitored, obviously the drugs are lost or diluted and this method cannot proceed. She then goes on to have a surgical abortion. She is advised against going on with the pregnancy because the residue of drugs could damage the child.

3) If the patient has not vomited, she is sent home after two hours. Twelve hours later half of the women will start to bleed and about 3% will abort at home. For the remainder, if in pain, no

aspirin or anti-inflammatory drugs must be taken for the eight to twelve days of the procedure, until after the last follow-up visit.

4) Two days after taking the RU486 the woman returns to the clinic. 97% of patients will still be pregnant. The prostaglandin, gemeprost, is then given as a vaginal pessary and a further 6 hours of monitoring is necessary. 90% of women will then abort painfully and it is during this time that recorded death and heart attacks have occurred. The UK Multi-Centre Trial (British Journal of Obst. and Gyn. June 1990, 'The efficacy and tolerance of mifepristone and prostaglandin in first trimester termination of pregnancy') showed that 60% of women needed painkillers, over half of whom required a morphine-type drug. These needed an extended stay at the clinic. The drug cocktail is now being further added to! Complications at this stage include: hypertension, heavy bleeding (1% needing curretage and blood transfusion) and acute pain. Gastrointestinal complications associated with prostaglandin include vomiting, nausea and diarrhoea. Fainting, fatigue and mood changes have also been noted. Even at this stage, 10% of women will not have aborted and will be sent home unless showing severe reactions.

5) 5-9 days after the prostaglandin is given, a follow-up visit is needed. If abortion is complete, the woman goes home. If not, a surgical abortion then takes place.

During all this time a woman's G.P. must be kept informed, and she must not be more than an hour's journey away from the clinic containing the resuscitation and other facilities. How can it stay confidential? Dare she risk telling no-one else if she may need swift transport back to the clinic? It might not be possible to use public transport if she is haemorrhaging badly. How long will she need off work? A fortnight's 'holiday'? Was all this explained to the women taking part in the National Opinion Poll who thought this method preferable?

In preceding chapters, women have told of the unexpected aftermath of feelings and problems following a surgical abortion, which takes place under anaesthetic, unseen or unheard by them, and all over in either a few hours or an overnight or at most a few days stay in hospital or private clinic. How much more will that trauma be compounded by the length, maybe sight, sound, or remembrance of the RU486 procedure? That is not to mention the possible physical consequences, some of which have been mentioned, some as yet unknown. Progesterone is found in other places in the body, including pituitary glands controlling all hormonal activity and in the central nervous system. Will this powerful drugs cocktail only attack the progesterone in the corpus luteum? What of other body supplies? Will it upset the entire bodily mechanism and interfere with the fertility of the woman in the future? What of its effect on any children she will subsequently bear? We cannot possibly know the outcome, nor can the 'experts', at this 'early' stage.

Edouard Sakiz, Chairman of Roussel Uclaf has said: 'As abortifacient procedures go, RU 486 is not at all easy to use. In fact it is much more complex to use than the technique of vacuum extraction. True, no anaesthetic is required, but a woman who wants to end her pregnancy has to "live" with her abortion for at least a week using this technique. It is an appalling psychological ordeal. We have only developed an alternative method of abortion, nothing more' (*Guardian Weekly*, August 19th. 1990).

Roussel Uclaf has stipulated that as a condition of continuing to supply RU486, users must supply them with details of efficacy and adverse effects on at least the first ten thousand women each clinic or hospital aborts in this way chemically. Are women the guinea pigs in a continued trial of this still experimental drug? It certainly looks that way.

There is already a system whereby a yellow card is sent to the CSM (Committee on Safety of Medicines) if there are adverse reactions to any drug. Every three months Roussel Uclaf reports the information from the abortion units back to the CSM. Why the double-check if this pill is proved and tested? In the early stages we were told that the pill was tried out on women in the Third World. Did they understand the implications? Would that be anything to do with the research into population control almost a quarter of a century ago?

Obviously abortion and contraception in the light of population control is another subject. Suffice to say that this earth provides, through God's creative power, enough food and resources to sustain its people. Even in this highly technological age, when we can fly swiftly to the other side of the world, or control spacecraft, we just have not spent the time and expertise needed on solving the food production and distribution problems, which are the cause of starvation and hunger. God continually creates and renews, while man often destroys, sometimes unintentionally. The whole history of the evolution of the drug RU486 points to an intentional destruction? Why? To 'help' women with unplanned pregnancies, or to solve a completely different problem with no thought for the woman's psychological or physical aftermath?

The complications after surgical or prostaglandin induced abortion are colossal and need money and resources to control. This DIY pill will only escalate the number of women with post-abortion syndrome and do nothing for the future health of the world.

'An appalling psychological ordeal', the manufacturer's Chairman calls it. Those who perform surgical abortions have never admitted that, yet we have seen the results. Why was this pill ever licensed anywhere, given that statement? Why have we allowed it into this country? It is not yet used everywhere here and many of us should let our local Health Authorities know what we think, hopefully before it ever gets to that stage. At the time of writing (March 1993) 2% of abortions in the U.K. are using RU486, but with an annual average of 180,000 terminations, this is 3,600 women victims each year too many. Some Authorities are using it on a trial basis. We need to keep at them too.

In France, one third of all abortions are said to be done by this chemical method. Reports from there suggest that some women go for the first three pills and once home, do not go back to the clinic. Do they think that the rest is not necessary and they will eventually abort? Or do they take fright when they are not one of the few who do abort within two days at home, then feel that they cannot go through the rest? For whatever reason, these women who fail to go back to the hospital or clinic are going on to have handicapped children. Reported cases are of babies born with deformed limbs, with both legs joined, etc., since the RU486 attacks at a vital stage of foetal development. The drug has to be administered before 42 days of pregnancy. (And how many women are exactly sure of their dates?) By the 12th week limbs are fully formed, but before 42 days it is a different story. To give birth to a handicapped child is one thing. To have deliberately caused that handicap because of an incomplete abortion is something else altogether.

Are women, especially those women who think the doctors are always right and who may not take too much heed of instructions, really aware of what a long and involved procedure of abortion they have chosen? Again, because the choice is there, women are having the freedom to choose the worse one, with maybe not nearly enough knowledge of what is involved. Some observers feel that the woman should have to stay in hospital, not go home for two days. If this happened, it would involve more expense, either for the woman in a private clinic, or for governments in state-funded hospitals. Women would then opt for the swifter, surgical abortion. What has been the point of developing this method at all? It will inevitably lead to more post-abortion trauma.

SUGGESTED WORKSHOP/
DISCUSSION GROUP/SEMINAR MATERIAL

1. Discuss:
Is the size of one's family a personal matter or should research into contraception and abortion be linked to population control? Do you believe that there are enough resources to feed everyone on the earth, or are these serious problems?

Bible work:
Read 1 Kings 8:37-43 and Genesis 41:14-40, 53-42:2. Are there any lessons we should learn from these passages?

Prayer:
For the hungry.
For Governments and projects, research and planning to counteract hunger.
For all Aid schemes and charities, that their staff and resources may be used wisely.
For those who study and research into population growth and control.
For those who manufacture and administer RU486 and other controversial drugs, that welfare will be put before profits.
For those who are suffering from PAS as a result of RU 486.
For those who are contemplating having an abortion using RU486.

Discuss:
What can we do to combat hunger and the use of RU486 as
a) an individual.
b) a church or group.
c) a society.
d) a world.

Close with the blessing.

CHAPTER 16

A NEVER-TO-BE-FORGOTTEN CHRISTMAS

After seeing a programme on TV praising RU486, one lady contacted LIFE, requested counselling and told her story. She had been one of the 1,000 British women on whom the new pill was tested. She had taken antibiotics for a routine ailment, and was not warned that these could counteract the effect of the contraceptive pill. She therefore became unknowingly pregnant. She visited her doctor just before one Christmas and tests were taken for the symptoms she described, including urine tests for diabetes. A few days later she was staggered to learn that she was pregnant. Because Christmas was so close, an appointment was made for 4 days later, by which time she and her partner were to have made up their minds what to do.

She says: 'I now realise that the options open to us were never fully explained, so from the moment I discovered I was pregnant, we never even considered the prospect of having a child. I believe that if I had thought it through I might have made a different choice. However, we talked it over with both sets of parents and decided on a termination.

'We both returned to tell the doctor after the weekend and were told "It would be best at this stage in your lives". Stemitil was prescribed for the sickness, but I was warned that once I had started to take it, if I changed my mind, the drug could affect the foetus.

'The hospital was informed, and I saw the consultant, with my Mum, 4 days before Christmas. He said that because it was Christmas, there would be no theatre lists until after the New Year. This would add 3 weeks to my pregnancy, but I could see another consultant who was conducting a medical trial on an "abortion drug".

'He explained that it would involve no stay in hospital, and because they said I was less than 8 weeks pregnant, it would be okay and it would be available to me the next day. He told me that I would enter the hospital for a 4 hour period in the morning and swallow three hormonal tablets, which would cause the lining of the womb to break up. During this time your blood pressure, pulse, temperature, etc. are monitored and then you return home. Two days later you return to hospital to have a prostaglandin pessary inserted. This would again involve a 4 hour stay for monitoring. Approximately four hours after this the lining of the womb would fall away like a period lasting 7-10 days. You would then return to the clinic for a check-up and that was it. So I decided to return the next day and have the RU 486. He didn't really explain the chances of the trial not being successful. He also said that I would have to fill in a record of how I felt each day.

'On December 23rd I was admitted into a day ward and given the three tablets, monitored for the four hours and allowed home. I was told how to fill in the charts. There were a selection of boxes to tick, ranging from O.K. to severe symptoms, including sickness, headaches, dizziness, bleeding, tiredness, flushing, etc. Over the next two days I still had the sickness but generally felt okay.

'I returned on Christmas Eve to the day ward, where they inserted the pessary and monitored me for four hours. I was picked up about 1.30 p.m. and went straight home to bed.

'I awoke at about 4 p.m. feeling extremely hot and as though I had begun to bleed. I tried to get out of bed to go to the bathroom, but as soon as my feet touched the carpet, I saw a huge pool of blood running down my legs and all over the floor. I fainted. The sound of my body hitting the floor brought my Mum and boyfriend rushing up the stairs. Both looked horrified as huge clots of blood and skin fell onto the carpet. I insisted that they carry me to the toilet. Once there I closed the door and must have passed out again, because I remember next that they were trying to hammer at the door to get in, but I was lying behind it. They eventually carried me back to my bedroom, but on the way across the landing I fainted again and smashed the corner of my face against a stereo unit. As I came round, I heard someone saying to call for an ambulance. I didn't really want this and I managed to persuade them both that I was just a little faint, but really inside I was petrified. I thought that if I went into the hospital, every one would be awful to me because of what I was doing.

'My Mum sent my Dad to the shops to buy some baby's disposable nappies, which was the only thing that could absorb the blood loss. I fell asleep and cannot recall anything else.

'On Christmas Day, I felt no sickness at all, but still had very severe bleeding. I continued to fill in the observation charts I had been given. I was due to return to the hospital on New Years' Eve. As the week passed, I felt physically a lot better, but I had begun to notice an offensive odour from my vagina and a strong, cramp-like pain in the pit of my stomach. I returned to the hospital and was told that it was procedure for patients to have a scan. When the nurse got a picture up on the screen, which I could see, she said she would have to fetch the doctor. When he returned, he then fetched the consultant, but no-one told me what was going on.

'Eventually the consultant told me that the RU 486 had not been successful and that I would have to stay in hospital right now and they would do an emergency evacuation under anaesthetic, because the foetus had not aborted correctly. In other words it had been a complete failure and I had suffered all that for nothing. I told them that it was impossible for me to stay there straight away and I offered to return at lunchtime the next day. They did not seem too happy, but agreed.

'When I returned home and told my boyfriend and parents what had happened, they could not believe it. Everyone was very sympathetic, but nobody could have understood how I felt then, only if they had been through it themselves.

'On New Year's Day, I returned to the ward at twelve o'clock and was booked in. Most of the nurses were great, telling me not to be worried and scared, but a couple of the older ones didn't understand how it was possible to get pregnant while taking the pill and couldn't figure out either why I had chosen to go on a medical trial, instead of a surgical termination. For some reason I wasn't given a pre-med., but they allowed my boyfriend to accompany me right to the doors of the theatre. Everyone there was very kind and explained what would happen whilst I was asleep. When I came round, I can't recall much until about 9 or 10 p.m., when I was given a lot of antibiotics.

'The following day the doctor who had performed the operation, came to see me and told me what they had found. Parts of the foetus were still adhered to the lining of the womb, and because it had been 7-10 days since the RU486, had begun to decay and caused an infection to set in. The infection was severe and that was causing the odour. He also told me that because the infection had been left untreated for over a week, there could be a 'chance' that I could be infertile. That was it. I was discharged home with two lots of tablets and told that if I wasn't happy with anything I was to go to my own G.P. I had no counselling and no support.

'Three years later, I suffered a nervous breakdown, some of which the doctors have blamed on the termination. I still had no outside counselling and I believe if it was not for the support of my parents and partner, I would not have been able to cope.'

As Edouard Sakiz rightly says, 'an appalling psychological ordeal', not to mention the physical pain at the time and the consequences afterwards. The results of those first British trials do little to reassure women. Of 580 women who went through the whole procedure like the lady mentioned above, 94% (553) aborted completely without surgery, but 6 % (35) required the same surgical evacuation of the uterus. Six of these were within 6 hours of having the prostaglandin, 4 because of haemorrhage and 2 because the RU486 was ineffective.

Of those who presumably went home and had to return, 5 evacuations were done at 1 - 5 days, 8 at 7 - 14 days and 13 at 15

- 28 days. No woman under 42 days pregnant required evacuation. This knowledge just makes the pressure on women to make an early decision even more intense. Nine women did not attend for follow up, so these were reported as successes.

But how is success measured? The results also show the percentages of pain, of excessive bleeding, of sickness and diarrhoea, they show that 28% required pethidine injections, etc., but mostly they show that this is not a safe, easy, well-tested and researched alternative to surgical abortion. Nor will it give women peace of mind afterwards. This lady suffered a nervous breakdown. Another case of post-abortion syndrome? Fortunately, her family knew of her ordeal and were able to support afterwards. What of those women who have no such support, who dare not tell their loved ones?

SUGGESTED WORKSHOP/
GROUP DISCUSSION/ SEMINAR

Read the story told in this chapter.

Discuss:
Is this practice valid in a so-called civilised society? Do you think this lady was told the true facts, or was that the simplest and best way for the doctor to explain it in order not to worry her? Take ten minutes to 'think yourself' into one of the people involved in the story. Write notes on how you think you would have felt, reacted, followed up the problem, etc. Compare with other members of the group and share ideas, feelings, intentions.

Bible work:
With the aid of a concordance, find any passages that you think would be relevant and say why.

Pray:
For all medical research, drugs trials and tests, that those taking part in them may be given the true facts.
For all those engaged in medical research that their thirst for knowledge may not cloud their humanity and judgement.
For all those involved in this story.
For pro-life counsellors and groups that they may be compassionate and caring, unjudgmental and unafraid to face problems.

Discuss:
How does this story affect us and what can we do, as: a) An individual.
b) A group.
c) A church.
d) A society.

Close with the blessing.

CHAPTER 17

ABORTION IS WORLDWIDE

Abortion and its aftermath is a worldwide problem. So far we have only looked at the after effects where the woman has had a 'choice', but another side to the story is the situation where women have no choice. State enforced abortion was the order of the day in Communist states in Eastern Europe. Today in China and in Tibet, amongst others, where each couple is allowed only one child, a further result has been the imbalance of the sexes. As John Cotter has written, 'Where Have All The Little Girls Gone?' With modern technology now able to give the sex of the child at an early stage in pregnancy, sex selection is another 'choice'.

Many women in the West, thankfully, prefer not to know the sex of their child beforehand, but for others, who want to plan, or who have to consider things like an extra bedroom needed if the child cannot 'double' with an existing family member, there can be the temptation to abort and 'try again', especially when not a first pregnancy.

In a USA study of 100 women who were told the sex of their unborn babies, 46 were carrying girls and 54 expecting boys. Of the girls, 29 out of the 46 were aborted. Only 1 boy was destroyed and 53 carried to full term. Another survey in the USA showed that 91% of women and 94% of men preferred their first-born to be a boy.

John Stephens, a Californian physician, offered sex screening tests to pregnant Canadian women. They flocked South , paying 500 dollars each to learn the sex of their child. Following that test, over 90% of babies aborted were female. (Canadian Pro-life News, Vol 17, no. 1. Jan. 1992.) Many of those Canadian women were of East Indian descent.

In Eastern countries, where there is a strong tradition of male dominance, sex selection h: . resulted in the destruction of so many female infants that the imbalance of the sexes will have a significant effect on the future. Many men will never find a wife and will be denied family life. For those who do marry, each young couple will have four elderly parents to care for at the end of their lives, with no other family assistance. The labour force will be equally imbalanced. Nikolai Dubinin, head of the Soviet Institute of General Genetics, has said, 'What we would have in the next generation then, would be about 90% boys and 10% girls. That would destroy everything for man ... his basis for emotion, for life. Everything would be destroyed.'

Sex selection takes on an even more sinister aspect when abortion is state enforced. If you are a Chinese father, naturally you want your one and only allowable child to be a boy. If you are a mother, you may realise that carried to its logical conclusion that could lead to the end of the Chinese species. How much psychological trauma are such parents subjected to even before they make a choice? What strain does it put on their marriages?

It can be argued that coercive abortion policy is against the fundamental human right of the woman to reproduce, apart from the fact that it imposes intolerable psychological damage. It can also be argued that enforced terminations and sterilisations are physical attacks on women and unborn children. They are crimes against women by a ruling power, yet those powers consider that to be pregnant is to commit a political crime. Much prayer and action is needed before women like this will be free of the psychological trauma of just being a woman! Maybe that is why some women concur with the decision to give birth to males only.

In some Eastern European countries, where women are at last being freed from enforced abortion, gynaecologists themselves are having to radically re-think their situation. When a LIFE team visited Latvia, members found hospital and medical school staff and students eager to listen and think through the pro-life stance.

Abortions have been legal in the Soviet Union, therefore in

Latvia, since 1956. Before then, 90% of abortions were back-street operations. This led to a 60-bed ward in Riga (Latvia's capital) being filled with cases of incomplete abortions and 12 women died every month as a result. After 1956, all abortions were free and allowed up to 12 weeks of pregnancy. In 1991 a charge of 50 roubles was asked, going up in 1992 to 150 roubles (80 pence at the time of printing), so merely a token charge. (The price of a decent meal for two people in a Riga restaurant! A gynaecologist in Latvia earns approximately £16 per month, if you want a further comparison.)

So-called 'medical abortions', that is the termination of pregnancy in the case of the child being handicapped, are allowable up to 22 weeks. Every gynaecologist must perform abortions and 52,000 are done each year. This is 125 abortions for every 100 live births, six times the rate of terminations in the U.K. When you consider that Latvia has a population about the size of Wales, the survival of the country gives sociologists a headache.

One gynaecologist, Dr. Mara Zake, who refused to do abortions was dismissed and is now in charge of a state-run orphanage, where she also cares for pregnant women. She founded a small pro-life Roman Catholic centre called Ave Maria, and is in touch with pro-life work in the USA. Pakapieni (Steps), an evangelical Christian Centre in Riga, run by William Schultz, is attempting pro-life work after the need was realised. William edited a Christian magazine of the same name and after writing on the pro-life theme, the staff became involved in pregnancy and post-abortion counselling. LIFE brought him to the 1992 national Conference, along with Dr. Sarmite Khartmane, Latvia's equivalent to our Minister of Health. She told how the powers-that-be turned a blind eye to falling birth-rates and increasing abortion, because under Communist rule the value of human life was very little. Since independence, Latvia has seen the need to survive and the Government has looked to Pakapieni for guidelines. If people like this could educate and enlighten, she thought that her people would be enabled to recover some of the old values.

Another gynaecologist, Dr. Maire Jansome said that many Latvian families used abortion as the basic means of birth control. In 1986 there were 137 abortions for every 100 live births! That may not be an accurate figure because all Latvian abortions are not registered. Many are still performed illegally. In the 1920s and '30s abortion was forbidden except to save the life of the mother. Catholic and Lutheran teaching was also influencing family life. Then came 40 years of Russian occupation and whilst people cannot be changed overnight, their 'soul' was destroyed and a growing generation had changed attitudes to life. For a time the birthrate increased, as low-educated and socially deprived families immigrated. Many of the more intellectual were either sent to Siberia or emigrated to the West. The idea that it was a crime to produce a child who would have so little opportunity in life was gradually accepted. There is virtually no family planning in Latvia.

One staggering statement Dr Jansome made was that changing the mind of the gynaecologist to a pro-life stance was easier in Latvia than changing the mind of the woman seeking abortion! There is a terrific work for Pakapieni and Ave Maria to do in Latvia. Educating the rank and file of the population is an absolute priority. William Schultz pleaded for pro-lifers in the U.K. to do all in their power to help. (More of this in the final chapter.) The Czech Lands have a similar experience. A Czech M.P. at the previous year's Conference, told of how she and members of her family had been imprisoned time and again for their pro-life stance under the Communist regime. A tiny figure in stature, but large in courage, she received a standing ovation after saying, 'In the words of St. Petra, it is better to suffer for doing good, than for doing evil. Those of us who had been Christians before the 40 years of Communist rule, knew that we just had to pray, live our own lives properly and wait. Christ went to the cross and overcame evil for all time. Communism could not last' (See 1 Peter 3:14).

With courage and faith like this, much can be done, but no-one can deny the enormity of the problems. Abortion is allowed on request and legal up to 12 weeks. After that, the woman's request requires authorization by a medical commission. For handicapped babies, however, abortion is allowed up to 26 weeks. The Government supports the use of contraception and 49% of married couples use it.

Abortion laws in Czechoslovakia were repeatedly amended, becoming more liberal each time. In 1950 termination was only allowable to save the mother's life. Illegal abortionists faced a penalty of ten years imprisonment, with one year for the woman involved. Because of the incidences of illness and death still arising from illegal operations, in 1957 the prison sentence was reduced to five years and the woman could apply to a panel of 4 doctors for a legal termination, but again, only for genuine medical reasons. Between then and 1983, the grounds for the permission were extended to those who were too young (under 16) or too old (over 45, later amended to 40, then to 35), those with too many children (3, later amended to 2). In 1987 the law was further updated and the commissions were abolished, leaving the decision between the woman and her doctor.

Abortion was always used as birth control because it was free and contraceptives were not. Now it has been reversed. Contraception, apart from condoms, is free, but there is an abortion fee chargeable after eight weeks of gestation. This places an intolerable burden on the woman to abort in haste, and repent at leisure! The number of abortions however increased after this legislation. In 1990, 160,000 terminations were recorded. In 1992 when the Czech Government made it harder for a woman to have an abortion, a charge of £40 to £80 was imposed for the operation, in a country where the average wage is £80 per month.

In Hungary, where there are 72 abortions for every 100 live births and where 90,000 babies were destroyed in 1990, the government has also been told to draft legislation to give more rights to the unborn child.

Bulgaria has one of the highest abortion rates in the world, with about half of all pregnancies terminated. It has been used as the principal method of birth control. It is allowable up to 12 weeks, but for handicap or risk of the mother's life being endangered, up to 20 weeks. The Government directly supports contraception, but only 7% of married couples use it. Between 1968 and 1990, the declining birthrate led to restrictions, such as no abortion for a first child, those with two or three were actively discouraged and unless for rape, handicap or risk to the mother's life, were almost unobtainable. In 1974 they were relaxed somewhat, allowing abortion for unmarried mothers, but still only in the first ten weeks. Since 1990, the rate has escalated. In countries such as this, where there is little artificial contraception, the field is wide open for education on the latest methods of natural and successful family planning, as advocated by many pro-lifers.

We have already mentioned France in connection with RU 486. There, 64% of women use artificial contraception. Before 1975 abortion was banned in France, then allowed up to ten weeks for a provisional five-year period, after which it was adopted as permanent. Although abortion figures have decreased since 1983, many French women have abortions in other countries (including the U.K.) because of the procedures taking time and the 10-week limit.

Once a woman has requested an abortion, she must consult a social worker or family counsellor, and renew her request in writing, but not until a week after the first approach. Where this would put the woman over the ten week limit, requests can be renewed earlier. However some doctors against doing abortions have been known to delay the permission. A change in the law at the end of 1982 extended social security payments to allow women 70% of the cost of abortion free. This provided a further incentive for the less well-off to make an early decision. Those aborting outside France would have to use private abortion clinics.

Belgium has a long history of fighting to legalize abortion. Fifteen attempts failed between 1971 and 1990, when it was finally allowed, up to 12 weeks of pregnancy.

Before that, legislation was based on the Napoleonic Penal

Code of 1810, adopted by Belgium in 1867 when she gained independence from France. It banned abortion totally, subject to 'the defence of necessity.' This was when three physicians certified that the pregnancy was life-threatening to the mother. Transgression of the law was severely punished and in 1923 additional legislation made it illegal to give contraceptive or abortion information.

The new law allows for termination when a woman is 'in a state of distress as a result of her situation'. The woman herself is the sole judge of her 'state of distress'. So in one piece of legislation, Belgium went from one extreme to the other. A woman has to be counselled after requesting abortion and must wait 6 days before finally giving her request in writing. 63% of married women in Belgium now use contraception.

Although abortion was illegal, before 1990 they were being performed on women at University hospitals and by private abortionists and clinics affiliated to the Action Group of Outpatient Clinics Practising Abortion (GACEPHA), a local initiative to provide abortion services.

Denmark banned abortion up to 1939, except for risk to the mother's life. By 1973 it was available on demand up to the first trimester (12-13 weeks). 96% of all abortions were approved in spite of the law. In 1973 it was allowable up to the twelfth week, and only thereafter if approved by a committee. Later this committee was modified to include a social worker and two doctors. Legal abortion increased after liberalisation, then decreased. There were 12.9 per 1,000 women aborting in 1972, increased to 27.0 in 1975. Then it declined, until it was 18.4 in 1984. Single women and women under 20 have the highest abortion rates. Around 60% of married women use contraception.

In Finland, where 77% of married couples rely on contraception to limit their families, abortion laws have been fairly broad since the 1950s, but were updated in 1970 with the upsurge of the women's liberation movement. Terminations are performed up to 12 weeks, except for risk to the mother's life or serious impairment of the child. 80% of abortions were performed on social grounds in 1982. The highest rate is among unmarried and younger women. As in Denmark, after liberalisation, the rate first rose then declined.

In Norway, laws are liberal for the first 12 weeks, then abortion is allowed for 'unreasonable strain' on the mother, difficult life conditions, etc. In fact, the usual 'social' reasons. It is illegal after 18 weeks unless for extreme cases. If the foetus is considered 'viable', i.e. able to survive outside the mother's womb, the abortion is not allowed. Pro-life work in Norway includes FLM (translated, The people's movement for right to life and dignity.) It is inter-denominational and courageously takes to the streets, with stands and literature handouts on the subject of abortion, euthanasia, sexual ethics, bioethical research and the rights of the handicapped to life. They also seek to educate in schools, churches and society in general.

Counselling services and practical assistance are given by AAN (Alternatives to Abortion in Norway). They maintain 24 pro-life centres.

FLM say that in Norway most 15-year-olds are confirmed in church. Ethical guidance on sex and lifestyle is part of confirmation course teaching. FLM has made a programme for two such lessons, including a video, literature, etc.

In the U.K. such teaching is usually confined to G.C.S.E. classes, if the pro-life group manages to be invited into the school. How much more suitable it would be as part of the Church programme for 'most 15-year-olds'! Whilst many schools welcome pro-life speakers now that abortion and euthanasia are on the curriculum, some teachers because of their own views or experience, are not accepting.

The pro-life world has been waiting with baited breath for news of Polish legislation. Since 1956 abortion had been available on demand in Poland up to the first 12 weeks of pregnancy. There were estimates that 600,000 to 1,000,000 were performed annually. However, in 1992 doctors followed an ethical code limiting abortions to 'extreme cases', and a new climate of opinion was introduced.

The debate has been waged heatedly in Poland for the past four years, and Lech Walesa has stated that he is personally against abortion and would never sign a law permitting it. However, he has now signed a law permitting abortion, (1) When the pregnancy endangers the mother's life, (2) after rape or incest, and (3) when prenatal tests show 'very serious or irreparable' damage to the baby. Social reasons were not considered justifiable. In cases of economic hardship, government bodies are urged to offer all necessary material help. Schools are obliged to teach respect for conceived life as well as guide youngsters towards good family lifestyle and responsible parenthood.

On the first condition, it has always been recognised almost worldwide, that abortion is allowable when the mother's life is in danger. Although this legislation is extremely restrictive by most countries' standards, the pro-life movement is disappointed that Poland was not able to give a lead to the rest of the world by saying that abortion after rape or incest is a double trauma and that the life of handicapped people is as precious and sacred as yours and mine. It would have been a fitting tribute to a Polish Pope.

At the moment, only Ireland is out of step with the rest of the world. The recent referendum confirmed the abortion ban, but information on abortion and the right to travel to other countries to obtain it is now allowed. Following the experience of a 14-year-old girl who was raped by a friend of the family, by whom she had been sexually abused for a long period, and who was not allowed to travel to England for an abortion, the case was referred to the European Supreme Court of Justice (which has described abortion as 'a service').

Here it was ruled that she could be given information and allowed to travel for the purpose of obtaining a termination of her pregnancy. This case obviously attracted wide publicity. It is not known if the young lady in question went ahead with the abortion. What we do know is that a young person who had been sexually assaulted over a number of years was pregnant. She was under the age of consent, therefore the man in question, whose identity was known to the family, was committing an illegal offence. The publicity never mentioned whether or not that man was ever arrested and sentenced for his crime. Instead, the young girl, who needed tender and skilful confidential counselling for the sexual abuse, not to mention the pregnancy, was hauled into the glare of media publicity, which must have compounded her trauma. Add to this a possible secret journey to a strange country for an abortion and one wonders whose interests were being promoted in the way in which this case was handled. Was it for her sake? Or to promote the cause for abortion in Ireland? Is she suffering, and still to suffer, after enduring the pain, indignity and secrecy of sexual assault in her childhood years, while the perpetrator has escaped scot free? Yet all the media attention was focused on the inhumanity of a law which denied her an abortion (and an added trauma!) The media is a powerful tool, but it can put a smokescreen over the real issues.

The Irish Government subsequently published a revised protocol to the Maastricht Treaty, which has signalled two major concessions on abortion and which will be sure to start another divisive campaign on this issue. The Irish Republic has already added a clause to the Treaty to guarantee that there will be no interference in the Irish Constitutional ban on abortion, but with the Supreme Court ruling and adverse reaction from several other EEC countries, the provisions to allow information and travel were initiated. Ireland votes on the Maastricht Treaty in a National Referendum in July 1993.

The situation in the USA since the inauguration of President Clinton, has been recorded earlier. With the growth of the pro-life movement during the Reagan and Bush administrations, when both presidents gave their support to it, many Americans were all set for sweeping changes to the present situation.

According to a report in *The European* (February 6th, 1992), a New York nurse has been teaching self-help abortion techniques since 1973. The method involves the help of at least three people. Interest rose when it looked as if the Supreme Court was on the verge of banning abortion. Under the new Administration, that does not now look likely. However, the nurse is reported to have said, 'This time, we will have to be able to take abortions into our own hands. If a need arises, our network is widespread enough to quickly share this knowledge with women throughout the country.' Mainstream abortionists have denounced the method. 'We believe it is dangerous to the health of the women we seek to assist,' said a policy statement from the National Abortion Federation. It is counter-productive to the aim of maintaining safe, legal and accessible abortion care.

Since the Supreme Court legalized abortion in 1973, over 20 million children have died by their mothers' consent. In the first ten years, one in four women is said to have aborted her unborn child. Abortion is a matter between a woman and her doctor during the first trimester. In the second, the state cannot stop an abortion, but can regulate which procedure is used. During the third trimester, the last three months, only life-threatening illness of the mother is grounds for termination.

With this 'help' for DIY abortions, plus President Clinton advocating that the Food and Drug Administration reverses its ban on the admission of RU 486 into the country, America could be building up even greater numbers of women with post-abortion trauma. The fact that it is a recognisable disease in the USA ought to be helping to decrease those figures.

Every minute, there are 105 abortions performed around the world. That is 6,278 each hour, or 150,000 every day. Human life indeed seems cheap and easily dispensed with in our 'throw away' age.

Abortionists in the West can say that post-abortion trauma is a guilt complex handed down from Victorian religious indoctrination and fostered by the pro-life movement, but there is just as much suffering in women who have been born and bred in Communist countries. On each trip to Eastern Europe, LIFE members have met them. New LIFE -styled centres opening in Prague, Bratislava and Riga are doing post-abortion counselling. Their women have had neither Victorian religious 'hang-ups' nor Christian or pro-life indoctrination. All they have in common with the women whose stories are documented in this book, is that they have had an abortion or abortions and have never been able to come to terms with the fact.

PART THREE

THE BIBLICAL PERSPECTIVE
AND THE CHRISTIAN RESPONSE

CHAPTER 18

WHAT THE BIBLE SAYS

The strongest argument for the value and credibility of life before birth is the fact that the life of Christ on earth began at conception. 'The Word was made flesh and came amongst us and we beheld his glory.'

The most unique event in history and the pivot of the Christian faith, planned by God with meticulous care, included life in the womb. The life of Christ started in the same way as each one of our lives began, except that Jesus was 'conceived by the Holy Ghost'. The Son of God himself came to earth as a conceptus.

This is so staggering, when you think of it calmly, in that it gives divine affirmation that this is where human life begins. It was in the power of God to be able to send his Son to earth at whatever age or in whatever way he wanted. Maybe the conventional idea was that he would come as a young priest to set the seal of God on all the religious observances of the day and then free his people from the power of Rome. Or they might have thought he would have come directly as a young warrior-lord, to head a mighty army and overthrow the occupation forces giving Israel her 'rightful' place leading the world.

Who would have thought he would come as a helpless baby, let alone that his time in the womb should be so well documented and linked with the Baptist even before birth!

In our technological and scientific age, we have proved beyond doubt that life begins at conception. However, for believers in previous generations, the events of the Annunciation, Mary's visit to her cousin Elizabeth and the birth of Jesus as recorded in the synoptic gospels, puts the seal on pre-birth worth. This book contains personal stories. Here's a 'paraphrase' of Mary's:

A devout God-fearing girl from a small village becomes pregnant, yet she has had no sexual relationship with her fiance, the local carpenter. For this 'sin', she could be stoned to death. Who would believe that an angel had told her in a dream that her child was to be the Messiah, God's chosen answer to the evil in the world?

Mary was a young woman facing a pregnancy before she was married, a pregnancy which she had not planned, and it was soon going to be evident to the village gossipmongers. Since Joseph, her fiance, was also a devout and God-fearing young man, and he knew that he was not responsible for her condition, he was wondering how he could whisk her away privately. (Matthew records the story from Joseph's viewpoint [1:18-25]). Maybe the visit to cousin Elizabeth was thought of in conjunction with Mary's mother. We don't know. We do know that Joseph also had a dream, telling him not to be afraid to go on with the marriage plans, because the baby was God's Son. For whatever reason, maybe because of village gossip, maybe because other relatives thought the dream was all in Mary's head and the pregnancy was a phantom one, she journeyed to see Elizabeth, who was well into her pregnancy with her first child, John, later to become the Baptist.

Elizabeth was getting on in years. Maybe Mary went just to help her, or perhaps her family did believe her and she was going to share her joy and the bond between them. For whatever reason, it seems that news of Mary's pregnancy had preceded her, including the dream sequence.

Because today we have had almost two thousand years of the story being told and retold, maybe we have lost some of the wonder and staggering implications of the narrative, told in great detail in Luke's gospel. It could only have been told by an eye witness. The most obvious one is Mary herself, telling it as it happened, remembering every detail of the conversation, as one does with momentous events in life.

Soon afterwards, Mary got ready and hurried off to a town in the hill country of Judea. She went into Zechariah's house and greeted Elizabeth. When Elizabeth heard Mary's greeting, the baby moved within her. Elizabeth was filled with the Holy Spirit and said in a loud voice, 'You are the most blessed of all women, and blessed is the child you will bear! Why should this great thing happen to me, that my Lord's mother comes to visit me? For as soon as I heard your greeting, the baby within me jumped for gladness. How happy you are to believe that the Lord's message to you will come true!' (Luke 1:39-45).

Elizabeth had also had the unique experience of hearing God tell her that, even at her age, when she thought she was past child-bearing, she was to be the mother of the Forerunner of the Messiah. (What a boost too for today's mothers who are made to feel uncomfortable because they are pregnant in their late thirties or forties!)

The 'Soon afterwards' of verse 39 is referring to Mary's dream, when the angel Gabriel announced to her the unbelievable news of her forth-coming motherhood. Soon after that, she hurried to the hill country. Maybe, again, before she told anyone else. She would have heard of Elizabeth's experience. Maybe she thought only Elizabeth would understand. Whatever the timescale of her going, she stayed for three months, leaving probably just before or just after John was born.

Another cause for wonder is that Elizabeth, who would by then have been feeling her baby's movements, says that when Mary arrived the baby jumped, or 'leapt' as the Authorised Version puts it, in her womb. Now that we know much more about pre-birth life, we know that Elizabeth's excitement would also affect her baby. Yet this seems to be something more. Elizabeth was 'filled with the Holy Spirit', filled with God's Spirit, and she remarks on the exceptional movement of her baby as he too seems to 'greet' Mary and the unborn Jesus.

The next wonder is that Elizabeth called Jesus 'My Lord', before he was born. Note the personal prefix, in a day when the general thought was that the Messiah would come for the nation as a whole, not to save individuals, yet here the language suggests a personal Saviour: 'My Lord'. Elizabeth, filled with God's Spirit, felt and inwardly knew something that thirty years later even the most learned rabbis failed to understand, that the Messiah had come to give his people personal freedom and peace, not a military stability. That would only come when everyone accepted the first requirement, to love God with all your soul, mind and strength and to love your neighbour as yourself.

Even though in later life Jesus himself did not specifically give any teaching on abortion, the whole of the Bible shows God to be pro-life in a personal relationship with his creation. The Bible is a book recording God's dealings with the people he has created. Because they had moved so far from the ideal way he had planned for them, he sent prophets and preachers, but finally, he had to send his own Son to show them the errors of their ways. From that time, he and his followers were promoting a 'kingdom of love' in the hearts of people, rather than a military strategy to conquer the world. Where the true love of Jesus has been demonstrated, peace has ensued.

Mother Teresa has said that abortion is the greatest deterrent to peace. When we think of 'the kingdom' as one of love and peace in people's hearts and minds, we see the answer to the lack of peace after abortion.

Terrified at heart and with no peace of mind, post-aborted women, as we have seen, often find their peace only in Jesus. Even as an unborn child, Elizabeth saw Jesus as a personal Lord and Saviour and re-assures Mary that her 'dream' was real and that it will come true.

Elizabeth and her cousin Mary would have been familiar with Old Testament writings of the child before birth.

Jeremiah, one of the prophets God sent earlier in the history of the Jewish nation, records: 'The Lord said to me, "I chose you before I gave you life, and before you were born I selected you to be a prophet to the nations." I answered, "Sovereign Lord, I don't know how to speak; I am too young." But the Lord said to me, "Do not say that you are too young, but go to the people I send you to and tell them everything I command you to say. Do not be afraid of them for I will be with you to protect you. I the Lord have spoken ... listen. I am giving you the words you must speak" (Jeremiah 1:4-9).

Not only does this show that God knows each unborn child in a personal way, but also that he has a purpose for each life. Elizabeth had been told what her child was to do. Mary knew that she was to have the honour and pain of giving birth to God's only Son, of rearing him and trying to follow God's plan for her own life. Jeremiah is told centuries before of his part in the purpose and planning of the Creator.

Was this just for great, unique men with special privileges? Obviously not, for we are told that Jesus was a man, human in every way as we are, except that he was faultless. Modern science tells us that we are human and unique from conception. At that point, a special blueprint, only as big as a pinhead, unseen by the naked eye, unfolds a spectacular sequence of events like a computer programme, that determines who and what we are.

At that moment the eventual size of our adult feet, the colour of our hair and eyes, our height and our natural tastes in music, our talents and our potentialities are determined.

Whether we develop those potentials and talents is another matter, but we can't alter the natural colour of our eyes or our height. Neither can we alter the fact, although we may chose to ignore it, that God created us in his own image and that he has maintained his interest in us ever since that unique moment when an egg from our mother and sperm from our father joined and began it all, as the Psalmist says, in an unseen place, hidden from human eye.

When we talk about disposing of the 'products of conception', this unique person is what we are talking about. When we talk of taking RU486 to make the environment hostile to those 'products of conception' this is what we are starving, unnaturally, as well as doing untold psychological harm to the mother who has been honoured to be given charge of this little life. God knows what he is doing, and however inadequate people may be in raising children, only when we get back to a new understanding of what conception actually means, will we have the responsible 'family planning' that God intended. Women like Mary and Elizabeth, women 'filled with God's Spirit', so close to God that they only ask that what he wills should happen in their lives, those women will take both the unplanned or the long awaited child as a unique gift from him.

We do not live in such a society, yet the work of the Church is always towards that aim, where the love of Jesus reigns supreme.

Way back in Old Testament days, unborn life in the womb was just as sacred. Ancient Hebrew law says: 'If some men are fighting and hurt a pregnant woman so that she loses her child, but she is not injured in any other way, the one who hurt her is to be fined whatever amount the woman's husband demands, subject to the approval of the judges. But if the woman herself is injured, the punishment shall be life for life, eye for eye, tooth for tooth, hand for hand, foot for foot, burn for burn, wound for wound, bruise for bruise.' So in ancient Hebrew law there was compensation for the lost life of an unborn child. No price was put on that child, but left to the discretion of the father, in the light of the circumstances, subject to the approval of the legal experts. That was in the event of a woman being accidentally caught up in either war or civil disturbance.

The prophet Elisha wept when he envisaged the future, we read in the Second Book of Kings.

"Why are you crying, sir?" Hazael asked.

"Because I know the horrible things you will do against the people of Israel," Elisha answered. "You will set their fortresses on fire, slaughter their finest young men, batter their children to death and rip open their pregnant women" (2 Kings 8:12).

The prophet Amos also proclaimed, 'The Lord says, "The people of Ammon have sinned again and again, and for this I will certainly punish them. In their wars for more territory they even ripped open pregnant women in Gilead" (Amos 1:13). They 'even' ripped open pregnant women. Here it seems as if the Lord sees this as the ultimate war crime, deserving punishment.

The prophet Isaiah records:
'But the people of Jerusalem said,
"The Lord has abandoned us.
He has forgotten us."
So the Lord answers,
"Can a woman forget her own baby
and not love the child she bore?
Even if a mother should forget her child,
I will never forget you!
I have written your name on the palms of my hands"
(Isaiah 49:15-16)

In God's opinion, it is unlikely that a mother will forget her own child. Here he is saying that mother love is one of the strongest of human emotions, yet even if a mother does sometimes forget her child, God never forgets his people. His love is stronger. Their names are engraved on the palms of his hands. This is one of the best examples he can give of his love, and he puts mother love as the human emotion most near to it and identifiable to it, for our finite minds to understand.

Even in the animal kingdom we see the strength of mother love. How much more so in humans, made in the image of God. Yet even when mothers 'forget' their children, God never forgets. Pregnant, worried mothers may temporarily 'forget' their child, even to the extent of aborting it, but God forgets neither that child nor that woman. Both of their names are written on the palms of his hands. When reason, fear, grief and guilt return, and the women 'remember' then God is still there, wanting to comfort and give his peace.

St. Paul says that our bodies are the temples of the Holy Spirit. The Jews and others of their day built 'temples' to house their God or gods. Paul says that each person can 'hold' the Holy Spirit, when becoming a Christian: 'Avoid immorality. Any other sin a man commits does not affect his body. Don't you know that your body is the temple of the Holy Spirit who lives in you and who was given to you by God? You do not belong to yourselves, but to God; he bought you for a price. So use your bodies for God's glory.'

The price God paid was the life of his Son, a priceless gift, yet God thought it worth it to save his children. In a day when we spend millions of pounds in money, hours of skilled labour and much patience in restoring and rebuilding man-made temples, churches, cathedrals, and the like from our past history, why are we not restoring and building up those temples of the Holy Spirit which have fallen into decay today? Those human 'temples' which need support today and will affect our future? No man or woman is an island. As we have seen, there is a ripple effect from abortion, both in families and in society. Many women will go through their lives in a state of collapse if they are not restored to their full potential. How much money, time, expertise and planning should we give to this? As a secular society, this is hardly being tackled, but as a Church, the challenge is there.

The Bible does not regard the unborn child as a blob of jelly or 'foetal tissue' or the 'products of conception', but as a unique human being, made in the image of God, with his provision, not only in that superb blueprint which will take care of its physical development, but also in the spiritual and moral provision needed for the future. God told Jeremiah that before he was born he had chosen him for a certain job. Like we all do when responsibility looms, Jeremiah said 'Oh no, Lord. I couldn't. I'm too young.' But God told him that he would give him the will and the strength and even give him the words to say, when he had to defend God's truth in a hostile environment.

Many pregnant women have said, 'Oh no! I couldn't! I'm, too young' or too financially insecure, etc. But when we do what we know is ethically and morally right, no matter how difficult, in the face of a hostile society, God will give the strength to carry us through. When God promised to send his Messiah, he says through the prophet Isaiah:

'Listen to me, distant nations,
You people who live far away!
Before I was born the Lord chose me
and appointed me to be his servant.
He made my words as sharp as a sword.
With his own hands he protected me.
He made me like an arrow
sharp and ready for use.
He said to me, "Israel, you are my servant;
because of you, people will praise me."

'I have a greater task for you, my servant.
Not only will you restore to greatness
the people of Israel who have survived,
But I will also make you a light to the nations -
So that all the world may be saved.'

(Isaiah 49:1-3, 6.)

Here, Jesus, who was acknowledged as Lord before he was born by Elizabeth, is promised as one who will 'restore' his people, who will be a light in the darkness, who will be able to save the whole world.

When we consider whether the Church should be using money, time and resources in supporting and helping to restore post-aborted women, we could be forgiven for thinking that it is a long, difficult and impossible task. When we read passages like those above, we begin to see that Jesus was chosen to save those women from the darkness in which they are groping. We also see that as his followers, who house his Holy Spirit in the temples of our bodies, we have the help that they need. We have the words they need because he has promised to supply them when we need them. Obviously counsellors still need training and knowledge, but the power and strength of the Holy Spirit is the motivating force and enabler for those who have the desire to help.

In the words of Psalm 22:31: 'People not yet born will be told, "The Lord saved his people." '

CHAPTER 19

WHAT THE BIBLE SAYS TO WOMEN WHO HAVE UNDERGONE ABORTION

If the last chapter has enthused any Christian readers to consider post-abortion counselling, note that while most women seeking counselling will have a vague belief in God as Creator, the majority are not church-goers. For those who are genuinely seeking forgiveness and have turned to the Church themselves, the knowledge that God has forgiven them will not bring about a dramatic change overnight in most cases. Intellectual reasoning is difficult for women who are going through psychological trauma. To know that something is true does not automatically affect your ability to change your behaviour in the light of that knowledge.

The counsellor needs to build up a relationship with the woman, whereby that knowledge will gradually become reality as she begins to feel herself a somebody, instead of a nobody, loved instead of rejected or judged, able to talk freely instead of having to keep a terrible personal secret. One lady told me, 'I prayed constantly for forgiveness and healing, but every service, every Bible reading condemned me more and more. I knew that God could forgive but I didn't think he could forgive me. I had destroyed my own child.'

Eventually, after I had listened and prayed for that lady for a time, I had to ask her why she was so special. Jesus had died for the sins of everyone, the Cross was wide enough and broad enough to cover the crimes of the most horrific mass murderer, if he repented, so why wasn't it big enough or powerful enough for her? She looked at me in amazement. The tears stopped momentarily. The whole root of the problem was that she could not forgive herself, therefore she could not accept God's forgiveness, even though she had told him many, many times how truly sorry she was. She also had problems with forgiving others involved in the abortion decision, including her husband. Her marriage had been under strain ever since, in spite of her beautiful three living children. She said every time they were at the table, she remembered there should have been four. She had to be gently led to grieve for her lost child and then let her go, giving her back to God, not trying to keep her in her home, at the lunch table, with her other children. That little girl would always be in her heart and that was right and proper, but Rachel had to come to the point where she stopped thinking of 'what might have been' and accepted reality.

We know that after any bereavement it is difficult to accept that a loved one has died. The hardest part is to give up that person into God's keeping and adapt to life without that special one. When women recognise that their 'foetus' was a lost member of the family, the next step is to grieve, then to let go.

We have already mentioned 'writing your grief behind you'. In 2. Samuel 1:17-27 we can read of David's lament for Saul and also for his best friend, Jonathan. He writes of:

'Saul and Jonathan, so wonderful and dear;
Together in life, together in death' (Verse 23).

and

'I grieve for you, my brother Jonathan:
how dear you were to me!' (Verse 26).

Jeremiah also found comfort in composing poetry and song:

'The prophet Jeremiah composed a lament for King Josiah. It has become custom in Israel for the singers, both men and women, to use this song when they mourn for him. The song is found in the collection of laments.' (2 Chronicles 35:25)

In 2 Samuel 3:31, David sang a lament for Abner and questioned his death, asking 'Why?' A typical reaction to a death.

Jesus said: 'Happy are those who mourn: God will comfort them' (Matthew 5:4).

At first glance the non-Christian will say, 'How can you be happy when you're mourning?' If you can mourn, your happiness will return, because you will be comforted. It is natural to express grief. Even Jesus wept at the grave of his friend Lazarus (John 11:35).

We could go on. The Biblical advice is that we need to grieve, not bottle up, blot out or try to negate our feelings. After abortion, women need to keep a diary, write a poem, write letters, talk to family and friends, if not, to seek out counsellors. The worst thing of all is to deny grieving.

Rachel believed with her head that she was forgiven, but could not accept it with her heart. The New Testament is just that, a new 'testament' or witness to the fact that Jesus has entered into a new covenant with his people, through his death on the cross. When we 'repent', are sorry and turn to him for help, his forgiveness is assured.

'And the Holy Spirit also gives us his witness. First he says, "This is the covenant that I will make with them in the days to come, says the Lord: I will put my laws in their hearts, and write them on their minds." And then he says, "I will not remember their sins and evil deeds any longer." So when these have been forgiven, an offering to take away sins is no longer needed' (Hebrews 10. 15-18).

God gave us memory. It is a most wonderful gift, bringing pleasure. However, when our memories haunt us, it gives us not pleasure but trauma. God has promised that once we are forgiven he will not remember our sins any more. From his point of view they are forgotten, finished with, deleted for all time. How futile then for us to go on, not only remembering them, but allowing the remembrance of them to so dominate our lives that it affects us, our families, our friends and our future relationships. Hard as it is, God asks that we let those bad memories go. He has disposed of them and so should we.

Then there is the anger. Rachel still felt angry with her husband and with the other people who had advised her and who had performed the operation. The Bible has a lot to say about anger: 'Jesus was angry when he looked around at them, but at the same time he felt sorry for them, because they were so stubborn and wrong' (Mark 3:5).

Those who pressurize women into abortion are usually either stubborn or wrong. The pro-life movement believes those who promote and perform them, however well intentioned, are wrong. A partner, parent, adviser, etc., can be very stubborn if they feel the coming child will interfere with their own plans, ambitions, comfort, etc.

Hard as it is, if we try to follow the example of Jesus, we see that his way is to feel sorry for these people, then show them a better course of action. In the events reported in Mark 3, Jesus was in the synagogue on the Sabbath day, where he met a man with a crippled arm. While he intended to heal the man for the victim's own sake, his enemies merely watched to see if he would perform a miracle so that they could accuse him of breaking the law. Although he was angry, Jesus soon showed them a better way. Sometimes a person's welfare is above the law. He performed the miracle and gave the man back his health, his ability to work and recover his self-respect and a more promising future. Jesus used his anger for good, not ill.

Even though the law of most lands today promotes abortion, those who oppose it are not trying to accuse those who take advantage of that law, but are working for their complete healing and renewing, whilst trying to show a better way for society to cope with the whole problem of sexuality and family life.

Jesus also taught that when we have something to offer to God, if we are angry with anyone, we should first make our peace, so that we are in the right frame of mind to approach a righteous God (Matthew 5:21-24). For those who are saying, 'I've killed my child!' note that in verse 22 Jesus is saying that being angry is just as bad as murder, if it is not 'righteous' anger but bitter or vindictive anger. With God, there are no degrees of sin, or of forgiveness. We do wrong. God forgives when we say sorry and deeply and genuinely mean it and intend not to do it again. It's as simple as that!

In Romans 12:14-21, St. Paul shows that God will be the one to judge or pay back for evil committed. We are asked to repay evil with good, to pray for those who wrong us.'

Hard teaching! But therapeutic, because as we begin to pray for people, we do feel sorry for them, as Jesus did that day with those who disagreed with his actions. They did not disagree with the man being healed, but with the healing being done on the Sabbath. That in itself was only a trap anyway, because they resented the power of Jesus. He saw through them. They were misleading their people just as women are misled when seeking abortion. Like Jesus, when we feel sorry for people and their wrong ideas, we can begin to understand them. Only then, can we show them a better way.

'And do not make God's Holy Spirit sad; for the Spirit is God's mark of ownership on you, a guarantee that the day will come when God will set you free. Get rid of all bitterness, passion and anger. No more shouting or insults, no more hateful feelings of any sort. Instead, be kind and tender-hearted to one another, and forgive one another, as God has forgiven you, through Christ' (Ephesians 4:30-32).

As people learn to forgive, so some of the bitterness falls away, the fear lessens, shifting the blame doesn't seem so important. Because the Bible is about people, and people do not change inwardly, these Bible verses are as relevant today as when each of them was first written. Human nature does not change, unless God is allowed to change it.

We read of depression in the Bible just as of guilt and grief: Jonah said, 'Now, Lord, let me die. I'm better off dead than alive.'

How often we hear that last phrase from women who have had an abortion and are in the depths of depression. Many admit that they have prayed that they will die. The ancient hymn writer so wisely said, 'Life is more solemn still than death.'

However, God says to us what he said to Jonah, 'What right have you to be angry?' (Jonah 4:3-4).

There follows in that chapter a curious little story about a plant. Jonah tried to build a little shelter in the shade of the scorching sun, then sat down and continued to dwell on his discontent with the way God was running the world and his life in particular. Jonah didn't think it fair that God should forgive the people of Nineveh for their sins, even though they had repented.

God still had Jonah's interests at heart, and up sprung a big plant, which gave more shade and made him more comfortable. But early next morning, a worm attacked the plant and it withered and died. Then the sun got up, accompanied by a hot wind, until Jonah was hot as well as bothered and again expressed a wish to die. Once more God asks, "What right have you to be angry about the plant?"

Jonah answered, 'I have every right to be angry - angry enough to die!' The Lord said to him, 'This plant grew up in one night and disappeared the next; you didn't do anything for it, and you didn't make it grow - yet you feel sorry for it! How much more then, should I have pity on Nineveh, that great city. After all, it has more than 120,000 innocent children in it, as well as many animals.'

Strangely, the Book of Jonah ends there! Strange though this little story is, it has a relevance to the whole question of post-abortion trauma. IT ISN'T FAIR! Of course it isn't! Abortion is not fair to the child, (and this story shows how God is concerned for innocent children), nor to the mother who may not have been told the true facts, nor to the staff who have to perform these primitive procedures, nor to those who have to pick up the pieces afterwards. But over and above all those considerations, it isn't fair to God. He is the creator of life. He caused that little life to be, to grow, even if only for a short time, for that mother. He is the one who has the real right to be angry, to be unforgiving, but if he forgives, has anyone else the right to argue with him?

Jesus had every right to be angry with those who falsely arrested him, charged him, tortured and eventually crucified him.

He went through the depths of depression and pain in the Garden of Gethsemane and again in that scorching sun, then torrential rain, on the cross, when he thought that even God had forsaken him. Yet at the end he was able to say, 'Father forgive them. They do not know what they are doing.' He could have been bitter and apportioned blame. There were many people to blame.

As we try to follow the example of Jesus and others as shown to us in the Bible, we will gradually lose not only our anger, bitterness, guilt, hatred and every other destructive feeling, but our wills will be lost into his and we shall then have that peace, that post-aborted women long for most of all.

As it says in Deuteronomy 30:19: 'Choose life, so that you and your children may live.'

Too late for women who have had abortions? Maybe, for some who have no further chance of motherhood, but for others, like Rachel, who have already sacrificed years of their lives to this trauma, their children will have fuller lives with a mother who has received Jesus and accepted his statement that he has come so that we may have life in all its fullness. Life in all its fullness is possible for every woman who has had an abortion. How sad that so few find it.

God has said, 'My people are destroyed for lack of knowledge' (Hosea 4:6). Jesus said, 'Father forgive them, for they do not know what they are doing.'

CHAPTER 20

THE CHRISTIAN RESPONSE: WHAT CAN WE DO?

If the whole question of abortion and its aftermath appals you, there is much that can be done. Some response will have come out of the workshop/seminar/group suggestions, if you have used these at the ends of the chapters. Some readers may have gone through the suggestions on their own, and will be seeking guidance for the future. It is therefore useful for us to look at what is already being done.

There are three main organisations which have been involved for many years on the pro-life scene.

LIFE came into being after the 1967 Abortion Act, aiming to do all in its power to rescind the Act. However when the full impact of the scale of the problem became apparent, a network of counselling offices were set up, giving free pregnancy testing and counselling. Here all the options were put to the mother, adoption and keeping the child being two positive ones, which often she did not hear about elsewhere. The next problem was accommodation for those who were planning to abort for that reason. Life members began to take such women into their own homes, then gradually a network of LIFE Houses were opened and run by volunteers. Today LIFE maintains 112 pregnancy care centres around the country, with a 24 hours a day telephone service, including ansaphones with numbers to ring in emergency, 54 LIFE Houses and a National Hotline for any woman who wants help when their local centre is not staffed, plus LIFE Baby shops, selling good quality second-hand baby and small children's clothing and equipment.

Last year (1992), the care service handled 91,520 calls for help

and hundreds of women were counselled for post-abortion syndrome as well as for crisis pregnancy.

Training is ongoing for counsellors, speakers and caring staff.
Local, regional and national training days and weekends are a
regular part of the work, to give all those involved the expertise and
credibility needed. Talks are given in schools, colleges, universities, hospitals, church or social groups, and on radio and TV
stations, as well as letters to the Press being written.

The U.K.'s first pro-life hospital is due to be opened not long
after this book is published. There is also a work going on in
Eastern Europe, but more of that later.

Throughout, LIFE has fought, through the legislative system to
get the law changed.

S.P.U.C. (The Society for the Protection of the Unborn Child) was
also in the pro-life fight early on. This organisation too does the
educational and political work needed to bring about a change in
attitude which will lead to new legislation. Although SPUC has no
residential homes, it does sustain a network of private homes
where women with crisis pregnancies can be accommodated.

It has a support group for parents of handicapped children, with
a Handicap Division, whose secretary, Alison Davis, was born
with spina bifida and works from a wheelchair.

On the educational side it also does extensive work in schools,
colleges, universities, hospitals and with all kinds of groups,
including talks to church groups.

Affiliated to SPUC Educational Trust, is B.V.A. (British
Victims of Abortion), co-ordinated by Bernadette Thompson,
herself a victim. BVA offers support to those suffering from PAS,
provides free one-to-one counselling and where possible, support
groups. They work with and refer to professional counsellors
where needed. They offer literature, (mailed discreetly on request)
and provide speakers for educational and political meetings. Like
LIFE, they conduct an ongoing survey to document the long-term
impact of abortion.

CARE (Christian Action, Research and Education) Trust also engages in the same scope of activity as SPUC, on the pro-life side, and is involved in the Sunday Trading Debate, the campaign against pornography and other issues, as they seek to promote the Christian ethos for home, family and society at large. Many CARE members form a network of caring homes for pregnant ladies, as well as for other victims of a secular society, who are hurting.

CARE too is looking into the long-term effects of abortion and its aftermath on individuals and society. It is only as these studies are done, as valid statistics and information is gathered and analysed, then published, that we can begin to convince women that abortion is not the easy option. At the moment, too many women are suffering alone and not realising that their experience can deter others from making the same mistake.

At the beginning of April 1993, a further off-shoot of pro-life activity, CHRISTIANS CARING FOR LIFE (CCFL) was officially taken over as a department of CARE. Many Christians in the south of England became concerned about abortion and set up Pregnancy Crisis Centres, beginning in Southampton with the Firgrove Centre, then in Basingstoke in East Sussex, and spreading out from these, more centres opened during the late 1980s. They became an association of Christian Centres, making up CCFL. Each one is independent, but they encourage each other, share resources where necessary, help new centres, hold conferences and seek to enlighten the Church on the issues of abortion. Co-ordinator Joanna Thomson of Basingstoke reports that there are 37 Centres as this book goes to print, with over 20 more in the planning stages. They continue to open in the South, but they are also flourishing in the North and Midlands. As the work expanded, it was realised that they needed a larger organisational base, hence the affiliation with CARE TRUST.

In her book *Even the Darkness* Carole Simpson tells of setting up a similar centre, CAFUL (Christian Action For Unborn Life) in February 1988. It became a Charitable Trust in early 1991.

Depending on where you live, what is happening locally, and what you would like to support, there is plenty of opportunity for Christians to get involved in pro-life work. Many are already involved in all kinds of other equally valid work, and, as always, it is a matter of what your own priorities are. If you are not able to be actively involved, any pro-life organisation will welcome you as a member and your annual subscription or a regular donation will help the work greatly.

If you do have time to get involved, going along to a local meeting should be all that is needed to get you started. Alternatively, invite a pro-life speaker to your Church or social group.

For those who want to be more actively involved, there is no barrier of age or sex. Every kind of skill is needed, from stuffing envelopes, to organisational expertise, from caring to counselling, from financial or secretarial skills to research, writing, speaking or promoting. If you are housebound and unable to take on any of this, you could still be doing the most valuable thing of all - *praying*. The organisation you choose will keep you well supplied with literature and prayer needs, whether it is for the LIFE Hospital, for their work in Eastern Europe or for specific needs of BVA, SPUC, CARE, CCFL or CAFUL. Whether promoting these needs in your Church prayer group or at home, pinning them onto the Church notice board or your own bedroom wall, you can play a vital part in the pro-life cause. Obviously, the more you can do the better, but do not despise the little jobs either. They all help to get the bigger things moving.

On the political front, since the Alton Bill and the Human Fertilisation and Embryo legislation, there has not been so much frontline political activity in Parliament, but still pro-life members are tackling their local, regional and national candidates on their stand on this vital issue. Your vote counts and your candidates in any of these areas will be interested in hearing the kind of person you would vote for. Therefore a letter writing ministry to M.Ps, local candidates, the local or national press, is another useful way of responding as a Christian. Your chosen pro-life organisation can give you guidelines on how to go about this. Maybe you feel unable to string a letter together, but you might have time on your hands to read newspapers and magazines and cut out relevant letters or articles that someone else in your church or group could deal with. Often the more active pro-life promoters do not have time to scour the Press and could miss out on local issues which need a pro-life response.

These are just a few suggestions as to the Christian response to the problem of abortion and its aftermath. They are equally relevant whether you live in the U.K. or anywhere else.

You may think that there is enough work to do in this country and you would be right. However, with the fall of Communism, a vast problem was recognised in Eastern Europe. Chapter 19 has touched on that problem. Two ladies, Maire and Jean, both LIFE members, one a recently retired doctor and the other a Headmistress of a girls' school, went on a motoring holiday in the summer of 1990. On the spur of the moment, they decided to cross the border into Romania to see for themselves what the situation was like. They were appalled! However, they did not just come home, talk about it and do nothing.

In just a few months, by the time the LIFE National Conference met in November of that year, they launched what they thought was a fund to make a one-off trip to Romanian orphanages with much needed medical supplies and whatever else they could take. To this end, in faith, a van was purchased and lettered, afterwards to be known affectionately as the Lifemobile. These ladies had a short slot, fitted into the busy Saturday afternoon programme in which they succinctly and effectively outlined the plan. Curtains were drawn to unveil the surprise vehicle, festooned with LIFE balloons and flanked by hotel Fire buckets waiting to receive donations. In an hour £6,000 was given or promised. By 10 a.m. on the Sunday morning, it had risen to almost £9,000 of the £25,000 needed to pay for the vehicle and finance the trip. This fund has been donated to voluntarily ever since. In the next two years, the Lifemobile made 7 trips to Romania, 5 to Czechoslovakia, 3 to Hungary, 2 to Poland and one to Latvia.

Pregnancy Care Centres, based on LIFE's U.K. centres, have been set up in Prague, Bratislava, Brno and elsewhere in Moravia. Life literature and its educational video have been translated into many of these languages. Life supplies have kept open a whole paediatric wing in one Romanian hospital. Thousands of pounds worth of medical supplies, food, clothing and literature have been sent, all because two ladies decided to go and see for themselves and do something about what they saw. The Lord multiplied the work and the money poured in, even in this country in a recession. As well as LIFE speakers and educators going to Eastern Europe, their representatives have been here, to see what is being done, as reported in chapter 19.

There is a terrific opportunity now for pro-life work to be promoted in the media, in Eastern European countries, with Communist controlled broadcasts and literature gone. However, many local Christians need help and guidance on media communication. In Hungary, the door was opened wide, then as more secular Western interests homed in on the programming, so it began to close. Where the door is still open, as in Latvia at the moment, we need to give all the help and encouragement we can to Christians struggling to promote a better way than the Communist abortion policy or the Western 'family planning' abortion programme.

Dr. John Ling, Secretary of Evangelicals for Life, the evangelical wing of LIFE, went to Latvia with the Lifemobile in 1992. He had never worked so hard in all his life! The party had been invited by a small pro-life evangelical charity called Pakapieni, an offshoot of a Christian magazine of that name. For a week in April he gave 18 lectures in hospitals, schools, colleges, nursing schools and churches.

John says: 'To go to a hospital and have 100 medical personnel turn out to hear a pro-life talk on Sex, Abortion and Life, is, to say the least, unusual. But in Latvia they came and they listened patiently and they questioned searchingly.'

John Ling and his party raced from city to city, town to town, and were overwhelmed by the sudden calls to go into radio stations and TV studios to give extra interviews and talks than had already been planned. As a result, LIFE flew five Latvian friends to the national Conference, as reported in Chapter 19. As is usual when a helping hand is stretched out, they gave back much to the Conference. From that first initiative by Maire and Jean, the enthusiasm, expertise, giving, planning, sharing and praying have enriched LIFE.

Just as with the beginning of LIFE work in Eastern Europe, plans for a LIFE Hospital seemed like an impossible dream. Again, funds have been set up extra to the normal pro-life work funded by members' subscriptions and donations.

Pro-life work is needed everywhere. The whole world is affected by abortion, because, as we have seen, most countries have legalised it. Ireland only has resisted so far. Wherever it has been legalized, wherever people think it is right because it is within the law, we have the problem of post-abortion syndrome. The most important Christian response is to offer the way of Christ to the nations.

'CHOOSE LIFE ... THAT YOU AND YOUR CHILDREN MAY LIVE' is a valid Christian call to the nations of the world today. That is the ideal, but what of the lonely woman, making a lonely decision about her just discovered unwanted pregnancy? What of her unborn child? To be ... or not to be....? that is the question.

TO BE ... OR NOT TO BE ...?
(With apologies to the Bard.)

To be or not to be ...?
That is the question,
That racks the hearts and minds
of those with unplanned pregnancy ...

Whether 'tis better to abort
these cells, this blob of tissue
that would inconvenience
her life and future issues?

To face the thought of parenthood
and all those 'seven ages',
the sleepless nights, the constant fight,
The awkward childhood stages ...

To be ... or not to be ...?
That is the question,
While legal Acts and doctors' facts
with Conscience are protesting ...

till she is led, like snail,
unwillingly to school
gut instinct, fool
maternal urge, curtail child's destiny.

To be ... or not to be ...?
'Tis life or death for one,
Then grief, guilt, pain for her
whose act can never be undone.

APPENDIX 1

Diagnostic Criteria for Post Abortion Syndrome

Developed by Vincent M. Rue, Ph.D. from diagnostic criteria for 'post traumatic Stress disorder', American Psychiatric Assoc., Diagnostic and Statistical Manual of Mental Disorders - Revised (DSM 111-R: 309.89) Washington D.C. American Psychiatric Press. 1987. Page 250.

A. *Stressor*: The abortion experience i.e. the intentional destruction of one's unborn child, is sufficiently traumatic and beyond the range of usual human experience so as to cause significant symptoms of re-experience, avoidance, and impacted grieving.

B. *Re-experience*: The abortion trauma is re-experienced in one of the following ways:

1. Recurrent and intrusive distressing recollections of the abortion experience.

2. Recurrent distressing dreams of the abortion or of the unborn child (e.g. baby dreams or foetal fantasies).

3. Sudden acting or feeling as if the abortion were re-occurring (including re-living the experience, illusions, hallucinations and disassociative (flashback) episodes including upon awakening or when intoxicated).

4. Intense psychological distress at exposure to events that symbolize or resemble the abortion experience (e.g. clinics, pregnant mothers, subsequent pregnancies).

5. Anniversary reactions of intense grieving and/or depression on subsequent anniversary dates of the abortion or on the projected due date of the aborted child.

C. *Avoidance*. Persistent avoidance of stimuli associated with the abortion trauma or numbing of general responsiveness (not present before the abortion), as indicated by at least three of the following:

1. Efforts to avoid or deny thoughts or feelings associated with the abortion.

2. Efforts to avoid activities, situations, or information that might arouse recollections of the abortion.

3. Inability to recall the abortion experience or an important aspect of the abortion (psychogenic amnesia).

4. Markedly diminished interest in significant activities.

5. Feeling of detachment or estrangement from others.

6. Withdrawal in relationships and/or reduced communication.

7. Restricted range of affect, e.g. unable to have loving or tender feelings.

8. Sense of foreshortened future, e.g. does not expect to have a career, marriage, or children, or a long life.

D. *Associated features.* Persistent symptoms (not present before the abortion) as indicated by at least two of the following:

1. Difficulty falling or staying asleep.

2. Irritability or outbursts of anger.

3. Difficulty concentrating.

4. Hypervigilence.

5. Exaggerated startle response to intrusive recollections or re-experiencing of the abortion trauma.

6. Physiologic reactivity upon exposure to events or situations that symbolize or resemble an aspect of the abortion (e.g. breaking out in a profuse sweat upon a pelvic examination, or hearing vacuum pump sounds.)

7. Depression and suicidal ideation.

8. Guilt about surviving when one's own child did not.

9. Self-devaluation and/or an inability to forgive one's self.

10. Secondary substance abuse.

E. *Course.* Duration of the disturbance (symptoms in B, C and D) of more that one month's duration, or onset may be delayed (greater than six months after the abortion).

APPENDIX 2

FOETAL DEVELOPMENT

Medical facts of how the baby develops in the womb.

Day 1. As the ovum and sperm meet in fertilisation, genetic make-up is complete. The sex, eye and hair colour, build and talents of a unique new individual are determined.

Day 19: The heart beats.

Day 24: Liver and lungs, etc. develop.

Day 28: Arms, legs, eyes, ears start to form.

Week 6: Skeleton complete and reflexes present. Liver, kidneys and lungs formed. Electrical brain wave patterns can be recorded.

Week 8: All organs functioning. Milk teeth and fingers, thumbs, ankles and toes formed.

Week 10: Sensitive to touch. Can turn head, frown, bend elbow and wrist independently.

Week 12: Capable of swallowing. Fingernails commence. Vocal chords complete. Inherited features can be discerned. (This is the end of the first trimester, when most abortions are performed.)

Week 16: Baby is half birth length. Heart pumps 50 pints of blood a day around the body.

Week 18: Responds to light, touch, sound pain.

Week 20: Hair, eyebrows, eye lashes appear. Can turn, suck, kick.

Week 28: Eyes open. Can hear mother's digestive processes and heartbeat.

Weeks 36-40: Birth ... just another stage of a well advanced process.

LIST OF HELPFUL ADDRESSES

BRITISH VICTIMS of ABORTION, Farnen House, 83, Abbey Rd., Barrow-in-Furness, Cumbria. LA 145ES
CARE Trust and *Christians Caring for Life*, 53, Romney St., London SWIP 3RF
CAFUL PO Box 108, Newbury, Berkshire, RG13 2HU.
LIFE House, Newbold Terrace, Leamington Spa, Warwickshire. CV32 4EA.
HOUSE OF COMMONS, Westminster, London SW1A OAA
SPUC, 7, Tufton St., London SWIP 3QN.

EXTRA READING

One Day I'll See You Jennifer Doe. Kingsway.
Will I Cry Tomorrow? Susan Stanford. Kingsway.
Even the Darkness Carole Simpson. OM Publishing
Timothy - Mission Accomplished Debbie Hill. New Wine Press
Birthright? Maureen Long. SPCK (available from the author)
Healing Memories David Seamands. Victor Books
Issues Facing Christians Today John Stott. Available from CARE Trust
Into the Arena Paul Miller. *Kingsway*
Love Minus Zero Alex Macdonald. Christian Focus Publications
The New Medicine The Rev. Dr. N. de Cameron. Hodder & Stoughton.
Abortion - A woman's Birthright? Noreen Riols. Hodder & Stoughton. (English Edition out of print French Edition still available.)